EUCHARIST *and* UNITY

A Theological Memoir

Keith Watkins

A Project of the Disciples of Christ Historical Society

Copyright © 2023 by Keith Watkins

All rights reserved. For permission to reuse content, please contact the Disciples of Christ Historical Society.

Cover image: ©Shutterstock
Cover and interior design: Connie H. C. Wang

Print: 9780827243439
EPUB: 9780827243446
EPDF: 9780827243453

Printed in the United States of America

Table of Contents

Foreword — v

Acknowledgments — vii

1. Looking for a Ritual to Join the Fragments — 1

2. Gathered at Christ's Table, Where All Are Fed — 11

3. Churches in Covenant Communion — 59

4. Churches of the Third Type — 99

5. Historian at Work and Play — 141

Bibliography — 175

Foreword

The early twenty-first century is an age of memoir. In the best memoirs the authors do not simply report autobiographical details but reflect on the meaning of their lives in the larger contexts in which they lived. The narrators consider how they responded to their worlds, including how they were shaped by their settings, how they transcended their situations, and how they helped shape their own moments and eras. The memoir writer provides pivotal factual data while bringing a broad range of perception into the narrative—feelings, insights, mountaintop experiences, frustrations, humor, poignance, deep fears, and hopes—sometimes cautious but sometimes bold. The best memoirs are not just about the person but about the communities in which the writer lived. Such volumes point the reader less to nostalgia and more to identifying the past mediated through the life of the author as a resource for understanding the present and moving towards the future in which readers can make contributions to their own times that are as appropriate as those set out in the memoir.

Keith Watkins, who taught Worship at Christian Theological Seminary for almost four decades, provides an exemplary memoir in these very ways. The book is structured around the major events in Professor Watkins' life, beginning with his childhood in the northwestern corner of the United States and discovering his life-long companion in marriage, Billie, in a Greek class in the basement of a congregation of a Christian Church related to the North American Christian Convention. More than rehearsing biographical details, Professor Watkins identifies and reflects on the theological dynamics at work in his worlds that led him towards the Disciples and into a scholarly career that began in church history and then brought the resources of that discipline and his emerging theology into the service of worship and into conciliar ecumenism and the search for a truly united (and uniting) church.

Professor Watkins was a prime mover at two levels. Among the Disciples, he was a leader in helping the church embrace the liturgical renewal movement with its emphasis on the Lord's Supper as the center of worship in the context of the Christian Year with the help of the newly emerging Common Lectionary. Less known among mainstream Disciples is the fact that Watkins was a force in ecumenical affairs more broadly. Professor Watkins is one of the very few scholars and leaders who were present at the births of these movements, who was deeply involved when they reached their height, who has continued to be a shaping force in liturgical renewal, and who is still an eyewitness to the changing nature and goals of what was conciliar ecumenism at its glory.

Aspects of Keith Watkins' story are shared by many in the Stone-Campbell Movement in the 1950s and 1960s as the Disciples and the North American churches gathered around their distinctive identities and missions. Although I am twenty years younger than Professor Watkins, and from the Ozark Mountains, I not only find elements of my own stories here but resources for helping me understand them.

Before closing, I want to emphasize the verve and clarity with which Professor Watkins writes. Unlike many tedious memoirs of religious leaders which are lost in a wilderness of arcane theological minutia, this book sparkles. It can become like a friend to anyone who joins Keith on its insightful retrospective journey.

Readers in the Christian Church (Disciples of Christ) will want this memoir for the insight it gives us into how the Lord's Supper in the context of liturgy is at the heart of our movement's life and mission. Readers in the broader Stone-Campbell Movement will want this book because it touches—with considerable sympathy—some of the important points of commonality and difference from the perspective of a Disciple. Readers in the Liturgical Renewal Movement and the conciliar Ecumenical Movement will want this book because of the clarity with which Watkins describes these phenomena from an insider's point of view. Keith was there. The last chapter of the book is a stirring testimony to his conviction that the witness to the gospel through the church, especially as expressed in worship and most especially at the Lord's Table, will continue to be a living resource for helping the world move towards the wholeness that God intends.

Ronald J. Allen
Christian Theological Seminary, Emeritus

Acknowledgments

I wrote the first draft of this theological memoir in 2002 but soon realized that it was not yet time to move forward to publication. Too much was still taking place in my post-retirement ministry. Nearly two decades later I revised the draft to bring it up to date and then shared it with a small circle of readers including Ronald J. Allen, a longtime colleague on the faculty of Christian Theological Seminary and still actively publishing in the field of Biblical Studies, and my son-in-law, Hebrew studies scholar Richard H. Lowery, who was soon to retire from his work as president of the Disciples of Christ Historical Society.

Ron immediately urged me to revise it for publication and, at my request, helped me reshape the manuscript. Rick told me about a series of books that the Historical Society was preparing for publication in partnership with Chalice Press, our church's publishing house. He encouraged me to submit the completed draft to his staff so that they could consider adding it to that list of books. Since my formatting skills are diminishing as I grow older, these two colleagues helped me locate bibliographical sources and enter them correctly into the manuscript. They encouraged me to keep going until it was ready for a final reading by the Historical Society's newly installed president, Joel Brown. Only then would it move forward to the copy-editing and design stages.

Although I take full responsibility for the text itself, these final services by Ron and Rick and the Disciples of Christ Historical Society have made it possible for me to complete this manuscript and let others move it the rest of the way to publication. Ron and Rick, I gladly express my gratitude for your personal encouragement and scholarly assistance in this process.

Peace and joy,
Keith Watkins

One

Looking for a Ritual to Join the Fragments

In 1953, the year I was ordained into the Christian ministry, the world was creating its post-war identity. While bombed out cities were being reconstructed, the economic and political forms of society were coming back together. Scarcely a decade later, this exuberant return to a state of super-normalcy unexpectedly went into a state of fibrillation. In the United States, the war in Vietnam, the rebellion of younger members of the society, and the Civil Rights movement were the most prominent signs of this erratic movement. In the 1970s, as the world returned to a more stable condition, everything seemed much the same, but everything was different. The form of the old remained, but the soul of the world had changed.

Perhaps the most critical year of that revolution was 1967–1968, during which Martin Luther King Jr. and Robert Kennedy were assassinated and many American cities were torched. With my family, I was living in Seattle, working as a visiting minister-theologian at University Christian Church. In a book I wrote that year, I quoted rock singer Jim Morrison who said, "I'm interested in everything about revolt, disorder, chaos, especially activity that has no meaning. It seems to me to be the road to freedom." Of Los Angeles he said, "This city is looking for a ritual to join its fragments." In response to Morrison, I implicitly affirmed the need for a ritual to join together the fragments of the cities but explicitly disagreed concerning the form that ritual would take. Instead of the "electric wedding" Morrison hoped to provide, I affirmed that what was needed was "the renewal of the Christian liturgy and the revivification of the basic wisdom that it expresses and communicates to the generations still to come."[1]

This renewal of worship—especially of the Eucharist, which is the church's central liturgy—for the sake of unity in the church and world has been the primary focus of my ministry ever since.

During the following decades, the political structures of the world moved through several stages, including periods of seeming stability between East and West and periods of ever more complex struggles between the regions and peoples of the world. It is hard to believe that, for a time, a certain level of peace and good will, with the United States leading worldwide alliances, prevailed. In our time the industrialized societies have achieved a brilliant technological civilization, but the price has been an undisciplined use of the natural resources of the earth. A Wordsworth poem that I learned in a high school English literature class has come true for Americans. Our preoccupation with "getting and spending" has "laid waste our powers. Little we see in Nature that is ours."

The tendency of Americans to equate social progress and economic growth has led to a civilization that has changed the world's climate, as though we were determined to bring about the apocalyptic promise that the earth will be destroyed by fire. At the same time, this determination to measure everything by short-term economic growth has led to the decay of once vital human communities, not only in the Developing World but in much of the United States, as can be seen in fishing communities on the Columbia River and farming towns in the Great Plains.

During the three-quarters of a century since my ordination, the churches also have passed through dramatic changes. Following World War II, they experienced rapid growth, and the historic Protestant churches consolidated their place among the mainstream institutions of American life. One sign of their prosperity was the erection of new buildings in communities all across the country. A series of theological movements—neo-orthodoxy, biblical theology, and process thought—crossed confessional boundaries and provided ways for Christians to talk about the events in the world. Although these theological schools of thought differed in their presuppositions, they all sought to describe ways in which Christians could respond

---

[1] Keith Watkins, *Liturgies in a Time When Cities Burn* (Nashville, TN: Abingdon Press, 1969), 28.

to the intellectual convictions of the scientific worldview and at the same time contribute to justice and mercy everywhere.

Under the leadership of Pope John XXIII, the Roman Catholic Church conducted the Second Vatican Council, which led to the transformation of that church and its opening up both to the modern world and to the mainstream Protestant churches. The liturgical movement, which focused attention on the renewal of worship, and the ecumenical movement, which brought separated churches into closer communion, became major preoccupations of church leaders around the world and in North America. Some of the most promising experiments in church renewal, such as the monastic community of Taizé, combined strong emphases on eucharistic worship, unity, and ministries in the world. As I continued my work, I found these communities to be exemplars of what I believed could happen in churches and communities everywhere.

Following the cultural crisis of the 1960s, however, churches found that everything had changed. Mainstream culture had cut a new channel, but the ecumenical Protestant churches seemed determined to continue their worship and work as though little had changed. By the mid-1970s, congregations and denominations around the country discovered that they were in a side eddy, slowing down into a state of stagnation. Meantime, churches that had slipped away from the American mainstream, including evangelical and charismatic churches, reached out to a generation that either had dropped out of the mainstream churches or had been outside of any church. Because these churches had not been in the older channel, it seemed easier for them to move directly into the new main current. The result was a dramatic shifting of the relative preeminence of churches.

When I began my ministry, I was learning how to sail in a church that at that time still seemed to be in the cultural mainstream. I had much to learn about navigating in these waters, and for nearly two decades I devoted much of my attention to learning the traditions and practices that characterized mainstream Protestant church life. By the time I had learned them, however, something had happened. The river had changed course and my ecclesial boat was in a side eddy rather than in the main channel. One way to understand my ministry since then is that it has been one person's attempt to move us out of the sluggish water into the swiftly flowing river; but despite the efforts of my generation, mainstream Protestant churches have not yet gotten past the sand bars that separate the old channel from the new.

I still think that this ecumenical Protestantism is the right boat for many citizens of our time who want to be in a church that is "spiritually alive, radically inclusive, and justice-oriented," to use the identity statement C. Kirk Hadaway and David A. Roozen proposed for mainstream Protestant churches.[2] We want to be in a church that is at home with the intellectual presuppositions of our time, tuned in to the art and music of the classical Western tradition, and prophetically engaged with the public sector and other social institutions. We continue to believe that this kind of church can help contemporary American society find a ritual that will gather up the fragments of our life and knit them into wholeness again.

This unifying process begins with the churches themselves, for our divided state is more a mirror of society's brokenness than an example of the wholeness we desire for the society of which we are a part. A major event in this process took place in a convocation in Memphis on January 20, 2002, when nine American mainstream churches established a new relationship they named *Churches Uniting in Christ*. In an extended liturgy, the churches recognized and declared that each of the other churches is a true church of Christ, exhibiting in its life the essential catholicity that begins with the New Testament apostles. They confessed the sin of division, reconciled separated ministries, prayed for the world, and then celebrated the Eucharist. As representatives of the churches partook of the one bread, they became one body, despite the fact that their separated ecclesiastical systems would continue to function. As a demonstration that reconciliation in American life—and in the churches—must include reconciliation across the barriers of race and class, the delegates to this convocation then joined a much larger procession of people who made their way to the Lorraine Motel, where Martin Luther King Jr. had died, and there they renewed their vows to overcome the injustice that still is so widespread in the United States.[3]

---

[2] C. Kirk Hadaway and David A. Roozen, *Rerouting the Protestant Mainstream: Sources of Growth and Opportunities for Change* (Nashville, TN: Abingdon Press, 1995), 88–89.

[3] The inaugural liturgy, articles, and addresses about the event and its meaning were published in *Mid-Stream* 44 (April/July 2002). I chaired the committee that drafted the liturgy.

The challenge now facing the churches is to live into the unity they declared and prayed for in the Memphis convocation. Although my work as pastor and professor is largely behind me, I hope to continue to be part of this process.

The title of this memoir—*Eucharist and Unity*—identifies the cause that has been at the center of my work as minister, teacher, and scholar: the relationship between worship and the unity of the church. I have tried to bring about a synthesis of the protestant spirit and the catholic substance of Christian worship in the conviction that this kind of worship will unite the church and help to heal the world. In the primary sense of the word, *catholic* means universal. The catholic substance of Christianity includes that which is essential to faith in Christ, celebrated in worship, normative for the church's life, and descriptive of the life of ordinary Christians. In a secondary sense, *catholic* means communion among the ecclesial communities that affirm a ministry in continuity with the apostles and a liturgical life based on the sacraments that are rooted in Christ's self-offering on the cross.

In its secondary sense, *protestant* refers to the historic churches that came into being during the sixteenth-century convulsion in Europe. The Enlightenment, the nationalism that led to the creation of the nations of Europe, and the desire for religious reform all came together. The international Roman Catholic Church was splintered by the breaking off of smaller churches that were largely identified with national boundaries—Lutheran in Germany and Scandinavia; Anglican in England; and Reformed in Switzerland, the Low Countries, and other parts of Europe. In its primary sense, *protestant* refers to the recognition that the church is, in part, a human construct and therefore lives in the alternation between judgment and renewal. This meaning of *protestant* explains the revival of preaching, the flowing of church music, and the democratization of leadership that emerged during ecclesial revolutions of the sixteenth century.

My efforts to reconnect the protestant and catholic aspects of the church have focused on the liturgical aspects of worship—on the shape and the spirit of the Sunday service and other occasions of worship, on the theology and form of the sacraments of baptism and eucharist, and on the cooperative leadership of clergy and laity in worship. I have been especially attentive to my own tradition—the Christian Churches, Disciples of Christ, Churches of Christ movement, now referred to as the Stone-Campbell movement—because we were the one ecumenical Protestant church that included the Lord's supper as a necessary part of the Sunday service. I rejoice in the achievements during this ecumenical era because the ecumenical Protestant churches and the Roman Catholic Church have moved toward a new consensus. Protestants have recovered much of the ecclesial catholicity that we lost long ago, and Catholics have embraced many of the protestant elements that this church long has needed.

Yet, I have come to realize with ever greater clarity that the mission of my life is even further from fulfillment now than when I started my work nearly three-quarters of a century ago. All around the world new Christian movements are coming into being, including new indigenous churches in Africa and Asia and new evangelical networks in the Americas. It is as though we have been piecing together a jigsaw puzzle and have reconstructed a fascinating section that depicts the church's ecclesial and sacramental features, only to discover that there is even more of the puzzle still to be worked on.

I now realize there has been a secondary motif in my efforts to meld the protestant and catholic aspects of worship. My growing preoccupation with the demographics of the church—the sharp decline of some churches and the rapid growth of others—has been an indirect attempt to understand how the churches can take the gospel to people in every class and culture. The church catholic reaches out to all people everywhere—to all kinds and conditions of humankind. Catholicity at its best has embraced all the people in the community where a church is located. It has found ways of accommodating its worship to the needs of the people, whoever those people might be. At first, the historic Protestant churches continued this demographic catholicity, and as long as the practice continued of there being only one kind of Protestant church in a community—whether Lutheran, Reformed, or Anglican—this quality survived. In the United States, however, these variations of Christianity, which in Europe had remained geographically separated from one another, were thrust into close proximity. Increasingly, Protestant churches became identified with specific ethnic or cultural groups. Even the post-World War II mainstream churches were identified with the economic and civic mainstream, whereas the rest of the society was aligned with other segments of the population.

It now seems clear to me, as it did not throughout much of my career, that the dramatic shift in strength of mainstream, Catholic, and evangelical churches expresses a shift in demographic catholicity. In the United States, the historic Protestant churches are less able to bridge cultural barriers than they used to be. They have lost a significant measure of the catholicity that is understood as the capacity to reach people of every ethnic and cultural condition. At the same time, the Roman Catholic Church and many of the evangelical and charismatic churches have figured out how to embrace a fairly wide range of classes and cultures. They have a greater degree of demographic catholicity than they used to have.

This book describes how I have come to a high degree of certainty with respect to one form of the catholic-protestant motif—that which deals with the church, ministry, and sacraments. This book also reveals that, with respect to demographic catholicity, I am uncertain and perplexed. If I were to have a second career as a professor of worship and pastoral leadership, the puzzles concerning the demographic form of the protestant-catholic motif would become more important than they have been in my first career. The second half of the century, however, has seen new divisions of the human family, some of them within the Christian community itself. It has witnessed terror beyond our ability to grasp and the rapid degradation of the natural world. The prospects for humanity seem bleaker now than at any time since the years of the plague in Europe. Now, even more than when I began my ministry, the world is desperately in need of rituals to bring it back together, and Christians must explore again their own system of religious rites and ceremonies to find a way of uniting the world again.

On the Sunday following the September 11, 2001, attacks on the Pentagon and the World Trade Center, large numbers of people went to churches and other places of worship. One of my family noted, as she described the service at her church, that at times of our deepest distress, the normal language of our secular lives is insufficient. It has neither the stories nor the testimonies of faith that we need to carry us through despair and tragedy back to courage and hope. My ardent prayer is that the churches of the world will continue to proclaim the stories of our faith and celebrate God's love for the world at the eucharistic feast, for this kind of worship provides a ritual to knit together the fragments of the church and the world.

I was born during the Depression, which was itself one sign of unresolved issues that led to World War II. The U.S. involvement in that conflagration began at Pearl Harbor, shortly after my tenth birthday. I was in the eighth grade at Multnomah Grade School on the outskirts of Portland, Oregon, on the day that President Franklin D. Roosevelt died. Our teacher was out of the room when the announcement of his death came over the loudspeaker, and I, feeling within myself that something had to be done, asked the class to stand for a minute of silence. At an all-years reunion fifty-six years later, a classmate whom I hadn't seen since we graduated long before, remembered that occasion, which was probably the first time that I assumed responsibility for public ritual. After four years at Lincoln High School in Portland, I attended Northwest Christian College in Eugene, Oregon, and then the Butler School of Religion in Indianapolis, Indiana. I served student pastorates in Dayton, Oregon, and Somerset, Indiana. A ministerial deferment kept me out of the Korean conflict. Following my theological studies, I became pastor of First Christian Church in Sanger, California, and then spent two years in doctoral studies at Pacific School of Religion in Berkeley, California, while also serving part time on the staff of Barrett Avenue Christian Church in nearby Richmond. During these years, the postwar return to religion was still taking place, but the surge was losing its strength and was soon to pass crest.

Midway through these studies in church history, I was invited to consider a position on the faculty of the seminary from which I had graduated. Since my departure from Indianapolis, the School of Religion at Butler University had become a separate corporation with a new vision and a new name—Christian Theological Seminary (CTS). The position was in the field of Christian ministries, and I was to teach courses that had been taught during my student years by Dean O. L. Shelton and later by Beauford A. Norris, who had been elected president of the seminary following Shelton's death. Because I had not undertaken any advanced study in worship or church administration, which were to be my areas of responsibility, I had much work to do in order to start classes in the fall of 1961. During my first three years as a professor, I not only organized my teaching responsibilities but also wrote my doctoral dissertation and drafted my first book. Upon the completion of my Th.D. degree in 1964, I became director of seminary worship in Sweeney Chapel, while continuing my other teaching responsibilities. In this new assignment, I was responsible for arranging a service of worship four days a week. The pattern long in place at the seminary was a simple form of morning worship—hymns, scripture, a brief sermon, and prayers.

On rare occasions I planned services at the seminary that attempted to unify the scattered elements of our city. The first celebrations of Martin Luther King Jr. Day in Indianapolis were in our chapel, with the integrated *a cappella* choir of Shortridge High School providing music.

I served on the faculty of Christian Theological Seminary until my retirement in early 1995, a career in theological education of thirty-three-and-a-half years. Although I carried several administrative assignments during those years, including two periods as acting dean, I continued to be primarily a teacher, with responsibilities for teaching worship and pastoral leadership. During my last years on the faculty, I carried the title director of Sweeney Chapel and moved my office to a location under the new chapel. It was much like being in a church office—with the sound of the organ in the background and the paraphernalia of worship surrounding me.

I was professionally active beyond the campus, serving as preacher and consultant in congregations, member of commissions of the Christian Church (Disciples of Christ), and participant in interdenominational activities, primarily through the Consultation on Church Union. One of the strengths of CTS throughout its history has been the way it has encouraged members of its faculty and staff to render service to the church and world as a significant part of their professorial responsibility. I published articles frequently in the seminary's journal *Encounter* and in other Disciples-related journals, including *Mid-Stream, Impact, and Discipliana*. I was a frequent contributor to the foremost U.S. journal on liturgical topics, *Worship*, published by St. John's Abbey in Collegeville, Minnesota. I wrote seven books on worship that were published either by Chalice Press or Abingdon Press and edited two more. Sales were never very high, and royalties on all of these books over my entire career totaled less than $20,000. Since retirement, I have published histories of CTS, the Yakama Christian Mission, and the Consultation on Church Union, and a book of dialogue sermons that I and three colleagues preached in Seattle during the year that Dr. King and

Senator Kennedy were murdered.

Writing for publication was integral to my teaching, and I understood it to be a way of extending my classroom and of engaging in serious conversation about worship with others in my discipline. Writing is an activity I have always enjoyed, and I am grateful for the love of good grammar and penmanship that was instilled in me by my parents and for the way that my first writing coach—Mertice Town, at Lincoln High School—set my course. Unlike many people, I have not maintained a personal journal of my experiences. Although I have kept representative course outlines for the classes I taught at the seminary, and notes or manuscripts for the majority of the sermons I have preached, I find that these documents are less helpful in understanding my work than are the essays and monographs I have published over some sixty years.

When I retired from CTS in the spring of 1995, I moved to Arizona to be the founding pastor of a new Disciples congregation—Mesa de Cristo Christian Church. I told people that although I was changing occupations—from professor to pastor—I was continuing the work that had claimed my heart and mind through all the years. The two years I gave to that venture were among the most important of my ministry, because they helped me clarify issues and understand more fully the challenges that face all of us who work for the health and wholeness of the church and the world. These two years, and later in interim ministries, also helped me understand with new clarity my own strengths and weaknesses as public leader of the church. I now realize the providential good fortune that was mine to live through a remarkable period in Christian history and to be able to enjoy freedom as a seminary professor to devote my entire professional energy to a single cause.

Two

Gathered At Christ's Table, Where All Are Fed

My earliest memory of attending Sunday morning worship is a day when my father took me, his four-year-old first-born, to church. My mother, who had been baptized as an infant at a Lutheran Church in a Finnish community in Minnesota, took us to Sunday school at the tiny Christian Church in St. John, Washington. I do not remember that Mother ever kept us for the brief communion service the church's elders conducted every week following closing exercises, nor did she stay for church on the occasional Sundays when a preacher came to town and conducted a preaching service following Sunday school and communion. Her three preschool children would have been a challenge. Although my father had grown up in St. John, his earlier religious activity had been in the Methodist Church, where he had for a time taught a Sunday school class. During my early years, however, he was not a church-going man.

The excitement I felt because my dad was taking me to church was matched by my fascination with the communion service. I was scarcely old enough to focus on the words and actions of the service—the brief interpretation of communion offered by the minister, the hymn sung by the congregation, and the prayers over loaf and cup offered by the elders. I had no preparation for the tray of small glasses filled with purplish-red grape juice. Even though Dad took the tray from the person next to me and handed it on it on to the next person without partaking, I could see the light shining on the juice and smell its strong aroma.

Although I may have been present for communion on a few occasions following that Sunday, I remember nothing more about the Lord's supper until we moved to the outskirts of Portland, Oregon, shortly before my tenth birthday. When a neighbor invited us to attend her Baptist church, Mother said that we belonged to the Christian Church. Because we had neither a telephone nor an automobile, the neighbor contacted the pastor of the Christian Church about a mile distant, in the village of Multnomah.

From that time forward we attended Sunday School and Morning Worship nearly every week. On most Sundays we walked the distance—nearly two miles—south on 45th Avenue to the abandoned interurban tracks, and east to the street that took us to the church. After the birth of the fifth and last child in our family, the pastor would drive out to get Mother and the two youngest children, but the rest of us walked the distance, Sunday after Sunday, as we attended church as faithfully as we went to school.

Morning worship at the Multnomah Church of Christ—the correct name of the congregation—was typical for congregations in the Christian Church movement[1] with a settled pastor. It began with several hymns sung by the congregation and a prayer offered by the pastor. Then came communion, introduced by a brief statement concerning the meaning of this ordinance, and a congregational hymn such as "Beneath the Cross of Jesus," during which the elders removed the white cloth that covered the trays for bread and grape juice on a table in front of the pulpit. Following brief extemporaneous prayers for the loaf and cup offered by two of the congregation's elders, the elements were passed through the congregation by the deacons. After communion, there was an offering, a longer prayer by the pastor, scripture reading, and the sermon. The hymn following the sermon provided an opportunity for people "to come forward," to confess faith in Christ in preparation for baptism by immersion or to transfer membership to the congregation. Early in our Multnomah years, the aluminum communion trays were replaced by trays made of myrtle wood, and the method of administration was altered. Henceforth, the trays of bread—matzo crackers that the elders had

---

[1] I am using the terms *Christian Church tradition* and *Christian Church movement* to refer to the ideas and practices that are characteristic of the movement begun by Barton W. Stone, Thomas Campbell, Alexander Campbell, and others in the early nineteenth century. This tradition is also referred to as the *Stone-Campbell movement*, the *Restoration movement*, or with variations of the terms *Christian Churches*, *Churches of Christ*, and *Disciples of Christ*.

broken following the prayers—were distributed and congregants held their bread so that all could partake together. Then the trays of cups were distributed, again with unison participation.

Following my baptism shortly before my twelfth birthday, I became a weekly communicant, a practice that has been foundational for my life ever since. The only instruction about the Lord's supper that I can remember from those years was typical for virtually all congregations of our movement. The one idea we affirmed was that in the Christian Churches and Churches of Christ—contrary to churches like the Methodist, Baptist, and Presbyterian—we observed communion every Sunday. If asked to explain its meaning, most people would have referred to the text engraved on the front of the communion table—In Remembrance—or cited language from one of the devotional hymns we sang in preparation for the service. The only time I remember attending the Lord's supper in a church other than one in the Christian Church movement was a nuptial Mass at St. Stephen's Episcopal Church in downtown Portland, when my sixth-grade teacher was married.

While I was still in grade school, I attended a revival meeting at our church and one evening went forward to commit my life to full-time Christian service, which meant that I intended to prepare for the ministry. My initial studies were at Northwest Christian College in Eugene, Oregon, followed by a three-year seminary course of study at the Butler University School of Religion in Indianapolis. Even in these schools, virtually nothing was taught about the history and theology of Christian worship and the sacraments. In general, my experiences and studies confirmed my childhood experiences at the Multnomah church. What little I did know about worship in the liturgical traditions had come from two monographs I read during my three-year pastorate at First Christian Church in Sanger, California, following graduation from seminary.

The first was a pamphlet by William Robinson, a leader of British Disciples and one of my teachers at the School of Religion, which he wrote to instruct elders of his own church concerning the principles, patterns, and language of the Sunday service. He had read deeply in the literature on worship and was well acquainted with the classic eucharistic traditions of the Church of England. He proposed a way for his Churches of Christ to worship that would be consistent both with their own past and with the classic tradition. Near the same time, I also read a new book on worship by Raymond Abba, a British New Testament scholar who, although from a "non-liturgical" tradition, was sympathetic with the new developments in worship.

Encouraged by these two writers, I was able to lead my congregation to revise its order of worship along the lines they were recommending.[2] The major revision was to rearrange the service so that the sermon came relatively early and the service culminated in the celebration of the Lord's supper. Almost immediately, I discovered that my preaching had to change. No matter what the topic, I now had to finish the sermon so that the congregation could celebrate communion. If I had learned that earlier in my ministry, the three years we spent in Sanger would have been far better for the congregation and much happier for me than they were.

During the Sanger years, my interest in worship was intensified by my work with junior and senior high school students in Northern California. As soon as I arrived at my pastorate in Sanger, immediately following seminary, I became part of a closely knit group of pastors brought together by Josh L. Wilson Jr., who was a member of the staff of the Christian Churches in Northern California and Nevada. Together we explored forms of worship for use in the region-wide youth events, especially the week-long conferences for youth leaders from the churches of the region. Wilson and I had become acquainted with innovative eucharistic liturgies being published at that time, and we worked seriously to adapt them for use with our adolescent worshipers in outdoor settings. My reading on worship and Wilson's experiences with a renewal movement called the Ecumenical Institute shaped our work. A note in the third edition of our project, published in the summer of 1962, reads, "this experimental liturgy has been edited and designed in the continuing dialogue regarding the liturgical renewal of the church."[3]

After three years as pastor of First Christian Church in Sanger, I was able to begin my doctoral studies at Pacific School of Religion in Berkeley, thus fulfilling the intention that had led to the decision to begin my full-time ministry in Northern California. With my family,

---

[2] William Robinson, *The Administration of the Lord's Supper* (Birmingham, UK: The Berean Press, 1947; reprinted, 1959). Raymond Abba, *Principles of Christian Worship* (New York: Oxford University Press, 1957).

[3] Josh L Wilson, Jr. (ed.). *A Recital of the Mighty Acts of God: An Order for Christian Meeting and Thanksgiving* (Berkeley, CA: The Christian Churches of Northern California–Nevada, 1962).

I moved to Richmond, California, a few miles north of Berkeley, so that I could resume my studies.

My intention to begin doctoral work was confirmed by a letter from Professor Ronald E. Osborn, who had just become the dean at my Indianapolis seminary, encouraging me to work on a doctorate in order to teach church history at the seminary level. I was financially supported, in part, by a teaching fellowship with Georgia Harkness, professor of applied theology, my first year and with John von Rohr, professor of historical theology and the history of Christianity, the second year. A part-time position with Barrett Avenue Christian Church in Richmond, primarily as youth director, provided a place for us to live and a small stipend. The two years at Pacific School of Religion initiated me into a more rigorous scholarly practice than I had previously known and socialized me into a much broader theological and ecclesiastical context than I had lived in previously.

Shaped by the Liturgy

Midway through my time in Berkeley, however, I was invited to the faculty of Christian Theological Seminary, but not in the field of church history. Instead, I would teach church administration and worship, but with the understanding that worship would be my primary area of responsibility. Because I needed to increase my knowledge of this field—in which I had already become interested but of which I knew very little—I took advantage of the presence in Berkeley of one of the foremost American authorities on the history and theology of worship: Massey Hamilton Shepherd Jr. of Church Divinity School of the Pacific. Because the course I audited was introductory and pastoral, Shepherd acquainted us with English language classics such as Gregory Dix's *The Shape of the Liturgy*, Evelyn Underhill's *Worship*, A. G. Hebert's *Liturgy and Society*, and Yngve Brilioth's *Eucharistic Faith and Practice: Evangelical and Catholic*. With considerable effort, I worked my way through these books, puzzled, sometimes put off, and yet half-persuaded. My difficulty with this literature was caused in large part by the fact that the ideas about worship they discussed were largely unknown to me. The only course in worship I had taken had been taught by Dean Orman L. Shelton at the Butler School of Religion, and it had been based on then-current Protestant writers like Willard L. Sperry and George Hedley.

One of those books Shepherd recommended—Gregory Dix's *The Shape of the Liturgy*—has been more influential than any other in forming my life as a Christian and my work as a professor of worship. A thick volume with dull green binding, it holds its place on many library shelves, often picked up but less often read, its heft too much except for the most determined readers. Despite the formidable character of this book, Dix has had a major impact upon liturgical revision—perhaps more than any other person in the twentieth century. He shifted attention from liturgical texts to the larger liturgical structures within which these texts function and demonstrated that the classic liturgies include basic components with later additions and developments. Dix taught people to identify Jewish roots in Christian worship. He gave readers a new way of understanding the development and character of the eucharistic prayer.[4]

Although Shepherd warned us that Dix was sometimes inaccurate in his historical references, he affirmed Dix's main ideas concerning the emergence in early Christianity of the church's worship at the table of remembrance.[5] I read other important monographs on the early development of Christian worship, but I kept coming back to a short list of ideas that Dix presented in striking language: (1) The distinctive form of Christian worship from the earliest times combines a service of the word and a service of the table with bread and wine. *Shape* is Dix's word for the sequence of major parts in that service, especially the actions at the table. (2) The prayer at the table was derived from Jewish sources and proclaims the meaning of the church's actions with bread and wine. (3) The purpose of the liturgy is a dynamic remembering of Jesus's passion and glorification, which enables the church to become in fact what

---

[4] A fuller description of Dix's impact on liturgical scholarship can be found in Byron D. Stuhlman, *Eucharistic Celebration, 1789–1979* (New York: Church Hymnal Corporation, 1988), 126ff.

[5] Gregory Dix, *The Shape of the Liturgy* (London, UK: Dacre Press, Adam & Charles Black, 1945). Despite its great length, *Shape* is organized in a way that helps novice readers. The major ideas are laid out fairly compactly in the first one hundred pages. The final chapter is perhaps the most eloquent characterization of the Eucharist in modern theological literature. The 625 pages in between provide vast detail and interesting, although often problematic, generalizations about the development of the eucharistic liturgy.

it already is in principle—the body of Christ. (4) This understanding of the Eucharist bridges the chasm that was cut by the sixteenth-century Reformation as the Protestant and Catholic branches of the Western church adopted opposing ways of overcoming the time lapse between the present and the "once and for all" sacrifice of Christ for the salvation of the world. Here Dix states in his own way ideas that had developed in the Roman Catholic liturgical movement and that were also being embraced by prominent Protestant theologians.[6]

For me, the most potent of Dix's ideas was his thesis concerning the emergence of the four-fold shape of the eucharistic portion of the liturgy. The day when Shepherd presented this idea in class was one of the momentous occasions of my academic life. Drawing on New Testament records, Dix states that at first the Eucharist consisted of seven actions based on Jewish ritual meals—three actions with a loaf of bread, a meal, and three actions with a cup of wine. During the first century, however, the meal was dropped, and the two sets of ritual actions were combined into one set—taking up the bread, offering a prayer of thanksgiving, breaking the loaf, and distributing both the bread and the cup to the worshipers. Hearing Shepherd describe this development, and then reading Dix's own exposition, I became convinced that this simple idea would be one of the cardinal principles of my work.

A closely related idea—perhaps it could be called a different statement of the same idea—is Dix's precise summary of the Eucharist. "The eucharist is an action—'do this'—with a particular meaning given to it by our Lord Himself—'for the *anamnesis* of Me.' The action is performed by the rite as a whole, the meaning is stated by the eucharistic prayer." The action, Dix continues, is fundamental, and it molds the prayer. Therefore, we begin by examining the shape of the rite, although always "in the light of the interpretation given by the prayer."[7] Dix uses the Greek word *anamnesis* in this statement because he believes that remembrance, the normal English equivalent, has too limited a meaning to convey Jesus' meaning. For the English

---

[6] Among the names associated with this theological movement are Odo Casel, Rudolf Otto, Max Thurian, and C. H. Dodd. An especially helpful summary of this movement is an autobiographical essay by Theodore Wedel, "The Theology of the Liturgical Movement." In Massey H. Shepherd (ed.), *The Liturgical Renewal of the Church* (New York: Oxford University Press, 1960).

[7] Dix, *The Shape of the Liturgy*, 238.

translations, he prefers *recalling*—which he hyphenated to bring out its meaning: *Anamnesis* is "the re-calling before God of the one sacrifice of Christ in all its accomplished and effectual fulness so that it is here and now operative by its effects in the souls of the redeemed."[8]

Although Dix develops this shape–prayer interpretive pattern to analyze the Eucharist, I have found that it is equally useful in examining other liturgical units. The interaction of shape, which is the carrier of a rite's action, and the principal prayer, which expresses the meaning inherent in the action, is fundamental to all acts of Christian worship.

As I was trying to find my way around in this new liturgical terrain, my part-time ministry in Richmond came to its close and I was free to attend other churches on Sunday mornings. The Bay Area of California provided many opportunities to attend worship in traditions that I had previously never experienced. Most notable to me were the eucharistic liturgies in the Hellenic Orthodox Church high up in the Oakland hills, and the services of Holy Communion at the Grace Episcopal Cathedral in San Francisco. Contrary to widespread practice in the Episcopal Church, Grace Cathedral invited baptized Christians from other churches to receive the bread and wine. Thus, I could attend worship there and experience eucharistic hospitality in addition to enjoying cogency of preaching and the splendor of music and ceremony. Palm Sunday 1961 was especially memorable because of the extended procession as the congregation sang, "All Glory, Laud, and Honor," and the dramatic reading of Matthew's passion narrative. I had never experienced anything like it—nor had my six-year-old daughter, Sharon, who accompanied me that day.

Another principle that henceforth would shape my work had come to me in November 1960 on the flight to Indianapolis to be interviewed for the teaching position at CTS. While on campus, I read an essay by Ralph Wilburn, who at that time was dean of another Disciples school, Lexington Theological Seminary. Near the end of his, "A Critique of the Restoration Principle," Wilburn asserts, "Disciples must develop more truly catholic attitudes," by which he means recovering a full sense of the church's heritage. Earlier in the essay he describes "a feeling for the catholicity of the church" as "a sense of the oneness with the total, historic continuum of the church through

---

[8] Ibid., 243.

twenty centuries," and he faults the sixteenth-century reformers and the Disciples' pioneers for breaking away from this catholicity.[9] Wilburn combines this affirmation of catholicity with a strong emphasis on continual transformation of the church's patterns of thought and ministry, thus preserving the values of the Protestant Reformation. The church for our time is catholic and reformed.

Wilburn's essay triggered an idea for the work I was hoping to begin at CTS. As I flew from Indianapolis back to San Francisco, I wrote out a draft of this idea that, with only slight revision, was published in the seminary's quarterly journal, *Encounter*. It was my first publication as a seminary professor. The pastoral challenge I addressed was the relationship between the approach to worship in mainstream Protestant churches such as Disciples and Methodists and the approach in churches such as Episcopal, Lutheran, and Roman Catholic. Whereas Wilburn dealt broadly with catholic and protestant as his categories, I used liturgical and free as the equivalent terms with respect to worship. My thesis was that we should create a new synthesis that brings together "the living center of the two traditions." Worship should be "liturgical in substance and free in principle."[10] I defined the liturgical substance as the coming together of the church "to celebrate the mighty acts of God in history," using the "full union of the service of the Word and the service of the sacrament."[11] Although the article does not include documentation, Dix's four-fold shape of the liturgy is part of the exposition I offered. The contribution of the free church to worship, the article concludes, is to insist on Christ's continuing lordship over worship as well as other aspects of human life. It insists on the importance of developing new materials and music and emphasizes the freedom that Christ gives the church. That conclusion still represents my deep conviction concerning the reform of worship that is important: "What can take place in our time is a return of the free churches to the mainstream of the church's eucharistic tradition. When they do so, not only will their own worship be refreshed, but the worship of the whole church will be renewed."[12]

---

[9] Ralph G. Wilburn, "A Critique of the Restoration Principle." *Encounter* 20, no. 3 (Summer 1959), 358.

[10] Keith Watkins, "Liturgy and the Free Church," *Encounter* 23, no. 2 (Spring 1962), 199.

[11] Ibid., 200–201.

[12] Ibid., 203.

Developing the Catholic Portion of the Synthesis

By the time I began my teaching at CTS, I had reached the central convictions about worship that shaped my work throughout my career, but my knowledge of the history and theology of worship, and of the new developments that were happening in the historic Western churches, was still marginal. The great challenge facing me as I began to construct syllabi for my courses was to acquire a fuller knowledge of the liturgical field. Half of my students would be Disciples and a fourth would be Methodist, with a rather wide mixture of other church traditions making up the remainder. From the beginning, I wanted students to find common ground in the biblical origins of Christian worship and in the classic tradition upon which their churches' liturgical patterns were built. Although it was important for all of them to become proficient in the traditions and practices of their own churches, I wanted to orient my students to the new approach to liturgical studies represented by the reforms that were taking place in the historic Western churches.

It was my good fortune to begin at a time of major liturgical reform in the churches that was generating a significant body of literature in a form I could comprehend and recommend to my students. Since 1950, the Episcopal Church had been publishing a series of small paperback books under the general title of *Prayer Book Studies*, each of which began with an essay discussing an aspect of the Prayer Book and then offered new texts or liturgical forms for study. During this same decade, five Lutheran bodies in North America were supporting the Inter-Lutheran Commission on Worship, which was publishing a similar series as one step toward creating a new service book and hymnal. Three Presbyterian churches were engaged in a similar process, as was the United Church of Christ. The Methodist Church was further along in its organizational process because its series of small books were understood to be the components for a trial Book of Worship that would become the official liturgical guide for the pastors and congregations of that church.[13]

The most complete rationale for these publications was offered by the Episcopal Church in the fifteenth book of their series, *The*

---

[13] More than fifty of these pamphlets and small books were published over a twenty-five-year period. The most important to me were those dealing with the Sunday service of word and table.

Problem and Method of Prayer Book Revision.[14] The "new liturgical knowledge makes it impossible to accept tacitly the English Prayer Book of 1662 as a definitive norm of liturgical unity in our Communion."[15] After citing the great difficulties in the previous method of revision, which was for a learned committee to make the proposals and for the church's highest authority to approve them, the book asserts that "a great liturgy is not merely an external, imposed law. It is a process welling up in continually fresh streams of devotion from the inner life of believing practicing Christians."[16]

These study books from half a dozen mainstream churches were much alike in their approach to liturgical reform and in their recommendations. They moved away from the norms that had been established in the sixteenth and seventeenth centuries and explored new historical and theological principles for reforming worship. They were aware of the liturgical ferment in the Roman Catholic and in their own communions around the world, especially in churches in Asia and Africa that had been established by their missionaries. As the norm for the Sunday service, they reaffirmed the eucharistic tradition of the New Testament that had continued in place until disrupted by the sixteenth-century Reformation, urging that congregations celebrate the Eucharist much more frequently than most were then doing. They recommended fresh language, and increasingly moved toward the use of contemporary forms of English rather than the archaic language that had been retained in churches. These books urged, it seemed to me, a way of worship that was remarkably faithful to the criterion I had already adopted for my own work—catholic in substance, free in principle.

My dean at the seminary, Ronald E. Osborn, aware of these developments among the churches, proposed that as a Disciple I could contribute to the discussion by preparing a draft order of holy communion for use every Sunday that he would publish in *Encounter*. His idea was that some of these churches might be persuaded to move in this direction but would find the recommendations of their own commissions unsatisfactory. After I had produced the draft, Osborn suggested that we send it to knowledgeable people in several other traditions and ask them to comment on the liturgy,

---

[14] New York: The Church Pension Fund, 1961.
[15] Ibid., 3.
[16] Ibid., 13.

with the understanding that these comments would be published with it. We agreed on the persons to invite, all of whom agreed to participate.[17] This liturgy and symposium introduced me to people working in the field of worship. It was cited in the recommendations for reform of the eucharistic rite in the Episcopal Church of the United States and in the creation of a new Anglican liturgy for Africa. Disciples' scholar and ecumenist W. B. Blakemore referred to it as "the most important single response of a Disciple to the concept of an ecumenical worship." In a comment that has turned out to be prophetic, Blakemore also said, "it remains to be seen whether Disciples in general understand its implications ... or whether they ... have within them the capacity for truly ecumenical attainment."[18]

With only minor revisions, I can still affirm the ideas in the introductory essay, but the liturgy itself falls short. Its *shape,* which uses the sequence of parts that have been the norm in most churches since earliest times, is satisfactory, but the language of the rite uses traditional liturgical forms that were becoming archaic. In preparing the eucharistic prayer, I drew on important new texts, including the acclaimed eucharistic liturgy of the Church of South India, but the theology expressed in my eucharistic prayer was couched in an idiom that even then was not congenial to me. Despite my efforts to be contemporary, the liturgy represents an era that was soon to be replaced by another. The enduring feature of the liturgy is the title I used for the eucharistic prayer: The Great Thanksgiving. I had seen the phrase in the commentary on an experimental liturgy, which had used "The Thanksgiving," without the adjective, as the title in the liturgy itself.[19] My use of the expanded phrase as the title for the eucharistic prayer is the earliest of which I am aware. In later years, "the great thanksgiving" has become commonplace in eucharistic liturgies.

The respondents came to much the same conclusion, affirming the principles and general character of the liturgy but making many suggestions for improving the rite itself. Offering a British

---

[17] Keith Watkins, "An Order of Holy Communion for Use Every Sunday," *Encounter* 24, no. 3 (Summer 1963). The symposium included responses from seven scholars representing Methodist, Anglican, Congregational and United Church of Christ, and Disciples perspectives.

[18] W. B. Blakemore, "Worship Among Disciples of Christ, 1920–1966," *Mid-Stream* 7, no. 4 (Summer 1968), 63.

[19] J. G. Davies, G. F. Cope, and D. A. Tytler, *An Experimental Liturgy* (Richmond, VA: John Knox Press, 1958), 45.

Congregationalist critique, Robert Paul concluded that this service, "would lead to sacerdotalism unless it were accompanied by a radical revision of our concept of the church and reorganization of our church life." He doubted that American Protestant churches were "ready for that kind of revolution, practically, emotionally, or spiritually."[20] In his extended, generally supportive critique, Massey Shepherd Jr. noted the absence of "the eschatological element—the looking forward to the realization and consummation of the kingdom." He also questioned the invitation to the table that I had borrowed from Grace Episcopal Cathedral—that all Christian people eligible to receive communion in their own church families are invited to partake. He did not see "that the indiscriminate inter-communion which so many Protestants practice, at least in inter-confessional relations, has contributed to a serious grappling with disunity, or has deepened in them a profound longing for that oneness in faith and witness which we know to be God's will."[21]

Especially interesting to me were the responses by two Disciples. G. Edwin Osborn, whom Disciples recognized as their leading scholar in the field of worship, affirmed my intentions but expressed his fears that younger scholars would move forward so quickly that "less agile" Disciples would not be able to keep pace, and that we would not be able to conserve "principles precious to us and essential to our witness." He could not agree with the idea of "a fairly constant eucharistic prayer," preferring extemporaneous prayers by lay elders, framed by "scripture readings which relevantly link the redemptive work of Jesus Christ to contemporary life, its issues and problems."[22] In contrast, W. J. Jarman, a pastor in Champaign, Illinois, stated that the most important aspect of the paper was "the change of viewpoint which it represents," setting aside both the Disciples' restorationist rationale and the psychological rationale (which G. Edwin Osborn used). Jarman's proposal, "based upon a prime interest in the unity of the church," was "to find an ecumenical consensus rather than to restore a New Testament worship." He stated that although my

---

[20] Robert S. Paul, "A British Congregational Critique," *Encounter* 24, no. 3 (Summer 1963), 320.

[21] Massey H. Shepherd, Jr. "An Anglican Critique," *Encounter* 24, no. 3 (Summer 1963), 323-324.

[22] G. Edwin Osborn, "A Disciples of Christ Critique," *Encounter* 24, no. 3 (Summer 1963), 326-328.

proposal might be impractical among Disciples at that moment, in twenty-five years—"with the ministers coming from our seminaries taught in the art of liturgy, and various congregations pioneering in the effort to bring a worship within a local church which reflects this ecumenical consensus"—Disciples could attain the principles expressed in the paper.[23]

While reading and writing about an ecumenical consensus in worship, I was also extending my experience of liturgical practice. Many Sundays during my first years on the faculty at CTS, I attended several churches in Indianapolis, especially Methodist, Presbyterian, Episcopal, and Lutheran. My exposure to worship reached a new level in 1965, when I was invited to participate in a new venture that was one of the first fruits of the opening between the Roman Catholic Church and other Western churches. Two scholars at the Vatican Council—Douglas Steere, a renowned Quaker leader, and Godfrey Diekmann, a Roman Catholic liturgical scholar—convened a group of Catholic, Protestant, and Orthodox scholars to reflect together on "the devotional side of religion."[24] The first conference took place at St. John's Abbey in Collegeville, Minnesota, which for a generation had been the leader in the liturgical movement of the Roman Catholic Church in the United States. This powerful community of Benedictines had a short time earlier dedicated a new abbey church, designed by architect Marcel Breuer, which was heralded as one of the great new ecclesiastical buildings in North America.

Each day began with Mass in one of the chapels of the great church. Although the non-Catholics were encouraged to participate fully in the liturgy, the table was closed to us, as the St. John's community could not violate the strict rules of the Roman Catholic Church. Each working session began with a prayer offered by one of the participants irrespective of denomination, and each day closed with a prayer service led by one of the Protestant or Orthodox participants. We ate together with the monastic community and were invited to participate fully in the daily prayer services of the monastic community.

---

[23] William Jarman, "A Disciples of Christ Critique," Encounter 24, no. 3 (Summer), 328–329. As I will indicate later, Jarman's forecast of the future has not been realized.

[24] Michael Marx, O.S.B. (ed.), *Protestants and Catholics on the Spiritual Life* (Collegeville, MN: The Liturgical Press, 1965), vii. These essays were first published in *Worship* (December 1965).

The several days at St. John's provided me with my first significant exposure to Catholic liturgy, culture, and life. It was transformative because for the first time I could experience some of the theological and liturgical phenomena that, until then, were things I had read about rather than realities I had experienced. Furthermore, it was my first exposure to a scholarly guild that was truly ecumenical and international. More than at any time in my previous activities, I found myself overwhelmed by the atmosphere, erudition, and energy of the event. I continued in the process for a couple of years, including a session at Douglas Steere's home base, Pendle Hill Retreat Center near Philadelphia. Because spirituality was peripheral to my primary liturgical interests, however, I dropped out after a time.

One significant benefit of this series of experiences was establishing a friendship with Michael Marx, who was the managing editor of *Worship*, the most important journal in the United States dealing with worship, and Godfrey Dickman, the senior editor of the journal. It was through their good offices that I began to publish in *Worship* as frequently as in *Encounter*.

My exposure to the liturgical movement was intensified in 1968, when I was appointed to succeed W. B. Blakemore as one of two Disciples representatives to the Commission on Worship of the Consultation on Church Union (COCU). COCU was moving forward with dramatic speed, in anticipation of bringing nine U.S. churches together into a new church that would be truly catholic, evangelical, and reformed. Each church was invited to send two persons to the worship commission; in addition, other churches not in the Consultation could send observer-participants. In this way, the commission included representatives of the Inter-Lutheran Commission on Worship, the Roman Catholic Bishops' Committee on the Liturgy, and the American Baptist Churches. At the time I joined the commission, it was the most important liturgical forum in North America, embracing young scholars like Methodist James F. White and Lutheran Hans Boeringer, and mature scholars like Massey Shepherd, Jr. Lewis Briner, a pastor in Kalamazoo, Michigan, represented the Presbyterian tradition. Louis Gunnemann, a seminary dean, and Howard Paine, a pastor, provided a steady presence for the United Church of Christ. My Disciples colleague was Colbert Cartwright, a Yale-trained pastor.

The dominant force, however, was Massey Shepherd, who was at the center of the Episcopal Church's liturgical forces, an active participant in the liturgical work of the Anglican Communion worldwide, and an accredited observer at Vatican II. Colbert Cartwright later described the commission as a "graduate seminar with Massey Shepherd the master teacher." By the time I joined the commission, it had nearly completed its work on, "An Order of Worship for the Proclamation of the Word of God and the Celebration of the Lord's supper, with Commentary,"[25] with Shepherd the writer. In preparation for my first meeting, I painstakingly examined the nearly completed draft the commission had been working on for several meetings and was ready to take an active role in the discussion. By that time, however, the draft was so mature that relatively little was changed. The preface stated that this liturgy was not intended to supplant existing liturgies of the participating churches, nor would it be imposed on the uniting churches. Rather, it was intended to be "a means of assisting us towards the common goal of understanding and reconciliation."[26] Although I do not find this sentiment in the published material, I remember vividly Shepherd stating his hope that nothing in the language of this liturgy would prohibit people from other traditions, including the Orthodox, from using it.

One of the important aspects of this liturgy was the committee's "endeavor" to "frame the prayers and devotions in a contemporary style of English, since this finds increasing favor in the newer liturgies in our several churches."[27] For such an early example of this transformation of language, the liturgy was surprisingly successful. Although the liturgy is marked by its time, it quickly became one of three or four pace-setting liturgies for the new eucharistic systems that the churches were creating.[28]

---

[25] The liturgy was adopted by the Consultation on Church Union in 1968 and published soon thereafter by Forward Movement Publications in Cincinnati.

[26] Ibid., 7.

[27] Ibid., 41.

[28] Four pace-setting liturgies are usually referred to as Church of South India, Taizé, Consultation on Church Union, and the Lima Liturgy. I discussed them briefly in Keith Watkins, *The Great Thanksgiving: The Eucharistic Norm of Christian Worship* (St. Louis, MO: Chalice Press, 1995), 33–36.

Redefining Free Worship

My approach to worship had a second element: the importance of maintaining freedom in worship. During my first three years on the faculty of CTS, I was writing my doctoral dissertation on the ecclesiology of Increase Mather, who was the dominant pastor during the second generation of New England Puritanism. My research led me to examine the major writings during the seventeenth and early eighteenth centuries in which radical reformers in the English Reformation, both in England and in New England, rejected "stinted liturgies" and advocated the use of extemporaneous prayers in all aspects of the church's public worship. Because I was teaching worship in a seminary where "non-liturgical worship" was highly prized, I paid close attention to this literature.[29] While working on American Puritanism, I realized that I knew little about the origins of worship in my own church and I began a concentrated program of reading in the early literature of the Christian Church movement, especially the writings of Alexander Campbell.

These activities came together nicely during the 1963–1964 academic year. A reduced teaching load at the seminary made it possible to concentrate my time on developing the first draft of my dissertation. During the interludes when my professors in Berkeley were reviewing my work, I had time to write the manuscript for my first book, which was published in 1966 with the title, *The Breaking of Bread: An Approach to Worship for the Christian Churches (Disciples of Christ)*.[30] My intention was to suggest an approach to "the understanding and practice of worship which takes seriously the Disciple heritage while at the same time it is responsive to the new movements in Christendom."[31] The first chapter presented a theology of worship that drew on literature from Protestant, Catholic, and Orthodox sources. Although my language was marred by the consistent use of the masculine gender, the ideas were consistent with the consensus about worship that had already become widespread among the historic churches around the

---

[29] Examples are John Cotton's *A Modest and Cleare Answer to Mr. Ball's Discourse of Set Forms of Prayer* (London: n.p., 1642), and Increase Mather's *Brief Discourse Concerning the Unlawfulness of the Common Prayer Worship* (Cambridge, MA: n.p., 1686).
[30] St. Louis: Bethany Press, 1966.
[31] Ibid., 8.

world. I also presented an explanation of the origins of the many patterns of worship, suggesting that the Catholic tradition was a unified stream—a mighty river like the Mississippi—that after the Protestant Reformation broke into many small streams, forming a delta by which the river reaches the sea.

In this context, I described and affirmed the free tradition as it had emerged in Puritanism. It was a way of worship that rejected prescribed services written in official books of worship and insisted that ministers and congregations, guided by Scripture and the Holy Spirit, should develop their own services and choose their own words with which to worship God. I then presented the historic Disciples' practice of worship as a variation of free worship, shaped by the effort to reproduce New Testament norms in the nineteenth century world and then to adapt their liturgical system to the changing cultural conditions of later generations. Disciples in our own time must continue the process of adaptation; but the major new factor we would have to consider was the worldwide liturgical movement. "In a way that has never before existed in Disciple history, we are forced to consider how the rest of Christendom worships before we can determine how we shall."[32]

This assertion led to a discussion based on the essay that had already been published in *Encounter*, urging that worship be "liturgical in substance and free in principle. The liturgical substance, I wrote, was the conviction that God is the primary actor in worship and the insistence that the classic service of word and sacrament—with the fourfold action at the communion table—is the way that worship should be arranged. These ideas fulfill Jesus' statement that we must worship God in truth.[33] Worship that is free in principle insists that our worship is continually under the judgment of God's "transcendent Word," open to "fresh incursions of the Holy Spirit," and ready to let the Spirit shape us as the Spirit wills. The church "must ever be alert to the critical review of past generations and to the creation of new liturgical materials." Furthermore, the church must reckon seriously with the people of our own time and their cultures. "To sum up in one word, worship that is free in principle is *alive*. It beats with the strong pulse of the young. It is full-throated, robust, pounding with energy. How could

---
[32] Ibid., 69.
[33] John 4:24.

worship be otherwise, for it is rendered by men [sic] who have been made alive in Christ!"[34] The book's final chapters developed specific implications for worship in Disciples congregations, using as an example a slightly revised version of the order that earlier had been published in *Encounter*.

Rereading this book a full generation later, I am surprised to see how fully formed my ideas were at that early period of my academic career. Even more, I am surprised by its energy and passion. This little book, scarcely 125 pages long, published when I was thirty-five years old, was my vision of the way Disciples could move—would have to move—in order to fulfill our role in the transformed world that was emerging.

As this book was developing, another process was creating a means to present these new liturgical ideas to Disciples. In 1961, the Disciples' International Convention, meeting in Kansas City, passed a resolution authorizing the appointment of a small study commission on worship and devotional life, "with the view of producing an interpretative statement about it, and of setting forth basic principles of public worship and devotional practice for our guidance." G. Edwin Osborn was the primary force behind this move, which was a mechanism to legitimize a process that had been begun by an informal fellowship of some thirty Disciples who were exchanging papers on the subject of worship.

Ronald Osborn's hope for the next stage in Disciples worship was expressed in a paper he had written for this group, marked as the second in the series, in which he declared that "Disciples are learning to worship." Osborn's main principle was that "any progressing culture gradually acquires more orderly ways to give expression to its history and character."[35] Thus, much of what was taking place in Disciples' worship was the proper movement toward order and dignity in the way that congregations come into God's presence. A second principle combined "Scripturealness [sic] and Psychological soundness" in order to determine the order and contents of a worship service.[36] The implications of these principles

---

[34] Keith Watkins, *The Breaking of Bread*, 79–84.
[35] G. Edwin Osborn. "Disciples Are Learning to Worship," 9. I am quoting from a copy of this article in the Cole Library of the Disciples Seminary Foundation, Claremont, California. I discovered it in September 2000, and do not remember having seen the article at any earlier time.
[36] Ibid., 13.

were developed in the service book Osborn had edited and which he interpreted in the final section of this paper.[37]

A key sentence was this: "The book has grown out of practices of worship among the Disciples, reflecting what we already are doing rather widely and well, rather than being an attempt to foist new or different forms upon a reluctant Brotherhood."[38] Osborn commended the Disciples' pattern of celebrating the Lord's supper "without a set liturgy." Most Protestants, he insisted, "have never broken completely from the Roman Catholic theology in connection with the Lord's supper, that it is an offering of the Body and Blood of Jesus Christ upon the altar in sacrifice to God to move him to grant pardon for sins, and to bestow his salvation and grace." The classic Disciples' way, in contrast, has taught that "the Communion is a fellowship with the Living Christ, Immanuel, a proclamation not alone of His death, but of His birth, life and teachings, of His resurrection, His return, and eternal purpose, and of the communicant's renewed loyalty to and identification with his Lord, receiving His grace and His Word."[39] In Osborn's book, the liturgical form for expressing this understanding is a framework of sentences and responsive materials drawn from the Bible, developing some 150 themes, connecting them to the Words of Institution and extemporaneous prayers of thanksgiving.

By 1965 when the committee was named, Osborn's declining health prevented his participation, even though he was listed as a consultant. The first meeting of the commission took place in 1966, with seventeen members, including the administrative secretary. Six of us were academics, four were pastors, four represented the arts and music, one was a mission executive, and another was a lay person with broad general knowledge of the church. Only two women and one person of color were on the team. Despite my inexperience in such matters, I was appointed chair. We met semi-annually for three years, with several members of the commission preparing papers that explored the Disciples' tradition of worship and the ecumenical framework within which decisions were being made.[40] In my introduction to these papers when they were published in

---

[37] G. Edwin Osborn (ed.), *Christian Worship: A Service Book* (St. Louis: Christian Board of Publication, 1953).

[38] Osborn, "Disciples Are Learning to Worship," 16.

[39] Ibid., 19.

[40] Six papers developed by the commission were published in *Mid-Stream* 7/4 (Summer 1968).

Mid-Stream, the journal of the Disciples' Council on Christian Unity, I stated that our intention was "to mediate the remarkable ecumenical consensus of our time to the congregations of our denomination so that their practice may increasingly reflect it."[41]

Harry Baker Adams, assistant dean at Yale Divinity School, was vice chair; and the commission persuaded him to draft our report to the Christian Church, which was published in 1969, after which the commission was dismissed. Coming from a distinguished Disciples family, Adams was deeply imbued with the history and ethos of the Christian Church movement and well-read in the literature on worship. Although his report drew extensively on the papers that had been developed by the commission, Adams incorporated his own insights into the draft that the commission adopted and published. The report referred to the liturgical and ecumenical renewals that were taking place, using them as rationale for Disciples to renew their own understandings and practices of worship. After defining worship as "a dynamic movement of God's action and man's response,"[42] it proposed criteria by which congregations could review and renew their worship practices. Among several "inadequate criteria," the report included the idea that there is a precise pattern in the New Testament to be used in determining worship in later generations. Yet the report affirmed the importance of "the thought forms and language of the Bible" as congregations arrange their worship.[43] It steadfastly refused to propose an order for Disciples to follow, but concluded with an extensive set of questions for use in congregations as they sought to renew their worship.

Altogether, the report, like its author, was calm, persuasive, and permissive rather than prescriptive. Its advocacy of ideas from the contemporary liturgical movement called on Disciples to move in directions most of them had never considered before. Although my language of "liturgical in substance and free in principle" was not in this report, its thrust certainly was consistent with the position I had been advocating. The commission's report brought this new mentality into the mainstream of our church's life.

A more accurate statement would be that the report *could have introduced a new perspective to the mainstream of our church's life.*

---

[41] *Mid-Stream* 7/4 (Summer 1968), 3.

[42] *Worship in the Christian Church: The Common Worship of the Church* (St. Louis: Christian Board of Publication, 1969), 36.

[43] Ibid., 48–49.

The fact is that, other than publishing our sixty-four-page study booklet, we had no strategy for taking these ideas to our church, urging them on our pastors and worship committees, recommending them to students in seminary, or moving them into places where important decisions about worship were being made. It is regrettable that we did not develop a process similar to those being used by other church bodies at the time. The booklet itself was equal in quality to the studies being published by Episcopalians, Lutherans, Presbyterians, and others. It was well adapted to the specific issues present in Disciples' history and practice. As the first phase in a concerted movement to renew and reform worship in our church, it could have had a significant impact on worship in the Christian Church (Disciples of Christ).

My confidence in these principles was confirmed by my experiences with University Christian Church in Seattle, during the 1967–1968 academic year. It was my first research leave, following six years of work at the seminary, and I was serving as visiting minister-theologian at this tall steeple church in the university district of Seattle. For many years this congregation had been one of half a dozen powerful Disciples' congregations in West Coast cities; although its membership had dropped significantly during the cultural turmoil of the 1960s, its cachet was still strong. Although we did not know each other, Pastor Robert A. Thomas had invited me to use that church as my base while I did the research and writing that would fulfill the terms of my leave. He was an impassioned Chicago liberal, committed to the church's engagement with the critical issues of the time, and bold in his preaching. He read his sermons, word-for-word, arms flailing, voice rising and falling in crescendo pattern, and despite his complex sentences, complete with many dependent clauses, he conveyed energy, enthusiasm, and life. The nine months that I sat in the pew listening to Thomas preach were the first time I had consistently felt excitement welling up as sermon time approached.

Although the service was conducted superbly, it was arranged according to the pattern that had emerged at a time when congregations celebrated the Lord's supper every Sunday but enjoyed preaching on an infrequent schedule. In this pattern, communion came early, and the climax to the service was the sermon. Early in the fall, Thomas and I debated a wide range of topics related to worship, and he concluded that it would be appropriate to suggest an experimental order to the congregation's worship committee. We discussed the various factors with that committee and with elders and deacons who would also be affected; then we interpreted the changes to the congregation. The trial period was several weeks during the late fall. When the time for evaluation came, the virtually unanimous decision was that we continue with the new order.

It seemed to me that what University Church and I were doing in Seattle was a harbinger of what could happen among Disciples all across the country. In the summer of 1968, when my family and I returned to our home in Indianapolis and I picked up my labors at the seminary, I was hopeful that real change could take hold in the congregations of the Christian Churches (Disciples of Christ). The liturgical change that had been made at University Christian Church was an example that could be offered to congregations across the country.

Mid-Course Complications

The greater part of my time in Seattle, however, was devoted to liturgical issues that were to become increasingly important as I picked up my labors in Indianapolis. The academic year 1967–1968 was the flash point for civil unrest in the United States and the cultural revolution that was taking place. During Holy Week, Martin Luther King Jr. was assassinated; a few weeks later, Bobby Kennedy was killed after winning the Democratic presidential primary in California. Because University Christian Church was located in the environs of the University of Washington, we were surrounded by hippie culture, resistance to the Vietnam War, and the assault on the American establishment. Although much of my time was devoted to studying the philosophy of symbolic forms, as developed by Ernst Cassirer and interpreted by Susanne Langer, I was much aware of the cultural and religious turmoil all around us. By late spring, I found myself ready to draw together what I had been reading, thinking, and saying throughout the year and, in less than a month, drafted the manuscript that was published as *Liturgies in a Time When Cities Burn*.[44]

In this book, I described the crisis we were experiencing, offered a critique of the conservative tendencies of churches, and provided

---

[44] Keith Watkins, *Liturgies in a Time When Cities Burn* (Nashville, TN: Abingdon Press, 1969), 115–120.

a defense of eucharistic worship, using my philosophical readings as the basis. My central claim was that Jesus of Nazareth portrays the nature of life itself, a tragic mixture of disappointment and hope, death and life. We sense that our lives, like Jesus's, "need not be crushed by the powers of this world that tower over us. Though we do not see God with our own eyes, we do see the man of sorrows whose death has brought new life to so many people."[45] I affirmed that the Lord's supper, celebrated in a theologically strong and culturally relevant manner, connects the people of our time with the one who represents God's triumph over the powers of this world. My commitment to ecumenical developments in worship and to the continuation of the free tradition was expressed later in the book urgently, in the hope that a new kind of church—with a transformed, eucharistic way of worship—would energize Christians for life in the world that was coming into being.

This belief that eucharistic worship could be a means of renewal in church and society was consistent with the findings of Alfred Shands, an Episcopal priest who was the founding pastor of a new parish in Washington, D.C. In the mid-1950s, he had spent time in England studying the liturgical movement and its implications for his own ministry in the United States. What he was finding was "a new depth of Christian life," directly connected to a theology that focuses on "the priesthood of Christ," which he offered to God eternally. In worship, Christians offer ourselves, "our souls and bodies through the eternal offering of Christ on behalf of the world."[46] The liturgy in the church pushes Christians into the world, where they continue this self-offering to God. Shands's book, which I discovered after returning to Indianapolis, confirmed in my mind the emphasis on transformed eucharistic worship that was the central theme of my Seattle-based book.

As I settled back into work in Indianapolis, however, I seemed to lose my sense of direction. During my absence, the chapel services on campus had been radicalized, in keeping with the movement to develop contemporary, celebrative forms of worship. Everywhere, the mood and methods of the Woodstock festival were being adapted for worship in churches and campus chapels. In a few places, such

---

[45] Ibid., 45.
[46] Alfred Shands, *The Liturgical Movement and the Local Church* (rev. ed.) (New York: Morehouse-Barlow Co., 1965), 16, 21.

as the Episcopal campus center at the University of Michigan, new music and expressive media were fused to the basic eucharistic liturgy; the result was liturgies that had theological depth and cultural immediacy.[47] In most places, however, the classic liturgical forms were scuttled, along with organs and sermons. At first, these changes at the seminary chapel had resulted in a dramatic increase in participation, but by mid-year the excitement had waned and attendance fell away. When I resumed oversight of the chapel, I tried to include both innovative and traditional services in the chapel schedule. It was not our custom to celebrate the Eucharist more often than once or twice a year. Despite my readiness to adapt our liturgical life to the new approaches, I failed to adopt the principles I had espoused so aggressively in *Liturgies*.

In 1970, the Disciples Study Commission on Worship was reconstituted for a second three-year term. Merrill Cadwell, Harry Baker Adams, and I were reappointed to the positions we had occupied previously; all but one of the other members were new to the commission. The members were chosen less because of special knowledge of liturgical matters and more because they represented various constituencies of our church. Congregations and pastors across the country were perplexed in the face of the demand for new forms of worship, and the commission decided that we could best serve our church by helping people figure out how to respond to the challenge of our time. We wanted to legitimize change and to help people make changes in responsible ways. Our report was published three years later, again with Adams as drafter, with the title *In Spirit and with Honesty*.[48] It was our effort to offer our church the guidance we were sure that it needed in such a confusing time.

Like our first report, *In Spirit and with Honesty* was gentle, positive, and encouraging. It provided a way to think about the rapid cultural and ecclesial changes that were occurring; but it offered little sense of urgency or promise. Furthermore, virtually no attention was given to the celebration of the Lord's supper. The book urged its readers to "Worship in truth. Worship in reality. Worship with honesty."[49] Yet it gave little help in how to do this. What would have

---

[47] Myron B. Bloy (ed.), *Multi-Media Worship: A Model and Nine Viewpoints* (New York: Seabury Press, 1969).

[48] St. Louis: Christian Board of Publication, 1973.

[49] *In Spirit and with Honesty* (1973), Council on Christian Unity, Christian Church (Disciples of Christ), 7.

happened to Disciples in later years if this commission had taken a more aggressive role, advocating the radical changes in eucharistic practice that both the ecumenical movement and the cultural revolution were demanding? This brief period in the early 1970s was probably the most important "failed opportunity" of my career.

During the years when the cultural revolution of the West was unsettling worship in the historic Protestant churches, the transformation of Roman Catholic worship continued. It had started a century earlier in Europe, inspired primarily by Benedictine communities and scholars. A central theme of this traditional liturgical movement was the reincorporation of the people into the church's liturgical celebrations. When the Second Vatican Council began its work, the foundations for transforming the liturgy had already been established. In 1963, the Council promulgated its first major document, the "Constitution on the Liturgy," which was sometimes referred to as "the new Pentecost for the Church."[50] In order to develop the implications of the Constitution, the Church appointed some forty commissions and working groups to revise the liturgies, including the Mass; create a new lectionary of Bible readings; and do everything else mandated in the new document. The rites were to be translated into vernacular languages so that worship would henceforth be in the living languages of the people. At the beginning of Advent 1969, Catholic churches in the United States changed from Latin to English as the language for celebrating the Mass.

Because of the Roman Catholic Church's international scope, size, and rich endowment of scholars and other leaders, it could engage in far more research and publication than other churches. Furthermore, accredited visitors were invited to observe and participate in the work of these committees and commissions. One person who did was Massey Shepherd Jr., and he readily shared his experience and insight with his Anglican colleagues and the members of COCU's commission on worship. His draft of COCU's eucharistic rite was influenced by these Catholic connections. Even more important was Shepherd's contribution concerning the lectionary for celebrations of the Eucharist. All of the churches that were developing new worship books in the early 1960s were planning to

---

[50] *Documents on the Liturgy, 1969–1979: Conciliar, Papal, and Curial Texts* (Collegeville, MD: The Liturgical Press, 1982), 3.

create new tables of Bible readings. At a meeting of the Commission on Worship, Shepherd proposed that the churches set aside their own lectionaries and, along with COCU itself, adopt the three-year Roman Catholic lectionary as the basis for their own. All agreed, and from that time forward, most of the historic Western churches have used variations of the same table of scripture readings.[51]

By this time in the 1970s, the excitement surrounding the Consultation on Church Union had diminished, but relations with Roman Catholic scholars and liturgical leaders continued to be one of the energizing aspects of work in the field of worship. Not the least of the reasons for me was the depth and excitement of eucharistic worship in their churches. Among my Protestant colleagues, I often found a certain indifference to the Eucharist; but among Catholics, the interest was always strong.

This strong sense of compatibility with Catholic worship was one of the reasons I decided to attend a liturgical conference at the University of Notre Dame in 1973. I was also attracted by the topic—ritual in contemporary American life—of which I knew little. The conference was, in part, a showcase for Aidan Kavanagh, a Benedictine monk from St. Meinrad Archabbey in Indiana, who directed the program in liturgical studies at Notre Dame. In presiding over the conference, Kavanagh demonstrated his comprehensive knowledge of everything related to ritual and worship ... and his potent wit. One speaker who caught my attention was Brian Wicker, an English journalist. He described the crisis in ritual behavior by asserting that attendance at university, which formerly had functioned as the ritual of initiation for young people in Western culture, no longer functioned this way because higher education had become so much a part of the world of business. The memories of the war in Vietnam were still vivid, and Wicker noted that a new ritualism was developing, shaped by the sense of taboo that had been so prominent in the resistance to the war.[52] Another speaker was Margaret Mead, who had achieved legendary status as an anthropologist interested in religious ritual. In contrast to

---

[51] A brief history of lectionaries and a series of interpretive essays about the three-year lectionary were published in *Interpretation* 31/2 (April 1977).

[52] Wicker's address, "Ritual and Culture: Some Dimensions of the Problem Today," was published in James Shaughnessy (ed.), *The Roots of Ritual* (Grand Rapids, MI: Eerdmans, 1973).

Wicker's precisely read lecture, Mead leaned on the podium and spoke to us in a warm, conversational manner. She described ritual in a broad and universal fashion and then noted how difficult it was for contemporary Americans to engage in ritual.

Although these lectures provided me a way of understanding the difficulties that churches were encountering in their worship, the most notable result for me from this conference was that it introduced me to the work of still another anthropologist—Victor Turner. A collection of his essays, entitled *The Forest of Symbols: Aspects of Ndembu Ritual*, had been reissued in paperback not long before and was available for purchase at the conference.[53] Although the book describes rituals in sub-Saharan Africa, Turner drew conclusions that could be applied much more broadly to human ritual behavior. The essays that most attracted my attention when I read them later in the summer seemed to have immediate applicability to my work as professor of worship, with special interest in the Eucharist.

Turner helped me understand the difference between two forms of human association—*communitas,* an intense community in which people work together on the basis of common inspiration, and *societas,* the more orderly, regulated community that gradually takes over as the inspiration of the immediate moment wanes. Turner also presented an idea that helped me understand the Eucharist. In many cultures, he wrote, color symbolism connects basic emotions generated in bodily experience to the values and behaviors that the community requires of its members. Red, which evokes the remembrance of human blood, is used to make people willing to sacrifice even life itself for the well-being of the larger society. Turner's ideas reconnected me to the bodily character of ritual, giving immediacy and passion to the abstract ideas of Cassirer and Langer that also continued as basic elements in my efforts to interpret the Eucharist.

I acknowledged this indebtedness to Cassirer, Langer, and Turner (and also to Gregory Dix) in the introduction to *The Feast of Joy*, a little book that was published in 1977.[54] I wrote it in

---

[53] Victor Turner, *The Forest of Symbols: Aspects of Ndembu Ritual* (Ithaca: Cornell University Press, 1970; originally published in 1967).

[54] Keith Watkins, *The Feast of Joy: The Lord's Supper in Free Churches* (St. Louis, MO: Bethany Press, 1977). Although this book, like all of my other books, sold only 2,000 to 3,000 copies, it remained in print longer than anything else I have written.

order to provide a new guide for Disciples pastors and elders, hoping it would replace the slender volume by Thomas Toler that had been widely used to train elders for offering prayers at the communion table.[55] I wanted to give a stronger theological foundation for celebrating the Lord's supper and better guidance in preparing prayers than was contained in Toler's book. Although one illustration referred explicitly to Disciples, the book as a whole was written so that it could be used by other churches with practices similar to Disciples'. Because the book was intended to be a simple, practical exposition, it has no footnotes. Throughout the text, however, ideas that I had drawn from my readings in ritual studies are prominent.

In the latter part of the book, I gave examples of scripture sentences, brief statements about the meaning of the Lord's supper, and prayers that could be used by elders. The prayers followed the four-fold outline presented earlier in the book—thanksgiving for new life in Jesus Christ; remembrance of his saving act for us, with specific reference to the bread and wine, which are "identified" with his body and blood[56]; calling on the Holy Spirit who unites past, present, and future; and rededicating our lives to God's service. These prayers represented what I thought Disciples elders might be willing to say at the communion table. Their strength is the variety of ways in which they express gratitude for new life, using language that is often biblical and redolent with classic themes of the gospel. Their primary weakness is the vague language at the point where the bread and wine are connected with Christ's body and blood. The strongest connection appears in the briefest of the prayers:

> Dear Father:
> Once again your Word has called us to the foot of the cross,
> where Jesus, strong of body and clear of mind, gave up his life for us.
> And now you invite us, when we eat this bread
> and drink from the cup of blessing,
> to receive again the benefits of his passion:
> forgiveness, a new beginning for life,

---

[55] Thomas W. Toler, *The Elder at the Lord's Table* (St. Louis, MO: Bethany Press, 1954).
[56] Keith Watkins, *The Feast of Joy*, 56.

and the indwelling power of the Holy Spirit to achieve that
life.
For these gifts we praise you.
At this table of remembrance we promise once again
to follow our Lord's example,
using our new life to help others come
to a fuller knowledge of Jesus and his steadfast love.
In his name we pray. Amen.[57]

I continue to believe there is a place among Disciples and more widely in the church for compact eucharistic prayers, similar in length to those in *The Feast of Joy*. The theology, especially at the sacramental center, needs to be stronger than in these prayers, connecting the bread and wine more explicitly to Christ's self-offering on the cross. In later publications, I use a pattern of words that is intended to strengthen this part of nontraditional prayers:

As we break the bread and drink from the cup,
may Jesus' own words be fulfilled:
My body given for you.
My blood of the covenant poured out for you.[58]

Over the years I have often offered eucharistic prayers—as an elder at University Park Christian Church in Indianapolis, where our family held membership; as pastor at the Federated Church of Homer, Indiana, and at the Mesa de Cristo Church in Surprise, Arizona; and as director of worship at the CTS's Sweeney Chapel. A later book dealing with Disciples' worship, *Celebrate with Thanksgiving*,[59] also discusses this kind of prayer and provides several patterns with examples. The longer I compose these prayers, however, the more challenging the task becomes. I understand why elders' prayers at the table are often devotionally strong but theologically weak, and I sympathize with elders as they try to fulfill

---
[57] Ibid., 120.
[58] I first recommended this formula in a booklet prepared for a series of workshops conducted by Peter M. Morgan, who carried the portfolio on worship for the Disciples' Division of Homeland Ministries: "The Communion Service: A Model for the Christian Church (Disciples of Christ)," 1983, 1985.
[59] Keith Watkins, *Celebrate with Thanksgiving: Patterns of Prayer at the Communion Table* (St. Louis: Chalice Press, 1991).

their responsibility, especially if they have had little training. I have reached the conclusion, however, that the 200-year experience of the Christian Church movement demonstrates that the practice of using fully extemporaneous prayers at the table—whether led by lay elders alone or with pastoral assistance—has resulted in a way of conducting the Eucharist that often is theologically weak and liturgically faulty.[60]

One exception to this statement is University Park Christian Church, which was our family's church home during our thirty-four years in Indianapolis. Over the years, I had helped the congregation develop an order for Sunday worship that exemplified the emerging ecumenical consensus. Many of the congregation's elders had developed patterns for their communion prayers that were more complete than those in most Disciples' congregations. In 1986, Leon M. Riley became pastor of the congregation and quickly demonstrated his liturgical sensitivity and skill. Within a few weeks, he added a brief post-communion prayer, which gave the service a devotionally satisfying conclusion. A more important addition was a prayer of thanksgiving by the pastor that consisted of a "brief recitation of salvation history, leading into the biblical words of institution and the recitation of the Lord's Prayer."[61] During his fourteen-year pastorate, Riley and the congregation continued to develop their celebration of the Lord's supper. The mature pattern included an invitation to the table spoken by the pastor, a communion hymn sung by the congregation, the receiving of the offering, and a brief song of praise sung by the congregation; a prayer for the offering offered by one elder and a prayer focused on the loaf and cup offered by a second elder; the pastor's prayer of thanksgiving, with some version of "Holy, Holy, Holy," or "Alleluia" sung by the congregation; distribution of communion to the people in the pews, with people eating the bread as it is passed and holding individual cups to partake in unison; prayer after communion; and a

---

[60] Keith Watkins, "Shifting Left/Shifting Right: Changing Eucharistic Practices in Churches of the Stone-Campbell Tradition," *Discipliana* 56, no. 2 (Summer 1996), 35–48, 64.

[61] Interview with Leon Riley, October 1, 2001. Riley subscribed to a monthly service edited by Robin Kash that included a full eucharistic prayer, which he greatly abbreviated for use at University Park Christian Church. He would use the same prayer for a month, except during special seasons of the church year.

recessional hymn. Riley's assessment of this order was that it carried the congregation and contributed a great sense of community that overcame the individualistic quality that has usually characterized celebrations of the Lord's supper in congregations of the Christian Church movement.

Although Riley's liturgical development at University Park Christian Church was consistent with my ideas, we rarely discussed these matters, and to draft his prayers he drew on resources that were unknown to me. After his retirement in 2000, he came across a paper on worship that he had written while a student at Pacific School of Religion forty years earlier. His footnotes recorded his strong dependence on "The Great Thanksgiving," which Josh L. Wilson and I had developed in our work with Disciples youth in Northern California–Nevada region. No wonder that I was so satisfied with the celebration of the Lord's supper under his leadership.

During the many years I have devoted to the Disciples' tradition of the Lord's supper, I have wondered why we have given so little scholarly attention to this important aspect of our life. An example of this inattention to our own history is the fact that we have ignored the close connection between evangelism and eucharistic worship at the famous Cane Ridge Meeting of 1801, which is regularly cited as one of the founding events for our Christian Church movement. Early in the 1970s, I read a contemporaneous account of the Kentucky Revival, including Cane Ridge, which reported that these revivals were "sacramental occasions," when large crowds of people came together for the celebration of the Lord's supper.[62] I discussed my discovery with Henry Shaw, a seminary colleague with extensive knowledge of Disciples' history; he said he had never heard that claim and doubted that the sacramental aspect of the camp meetings had any significance.

Despite Shaw's skepticism, I began to watch for other evidence that might clarify this matter. During a research leave in 1982–1983 at the Graduate Theological Union in Berkeley, I devoted a serious block of time to investigating the topic. To my amazement,

---

[62] William W. Woodward, *Surprising Accounts of the Revival of Religion: 1802*, excerpted in H. Shelton Smith, Robert T. Handy, and Lefferts A. Loetscher (eds.), *American Christianity* (vol. I) (New York: Charles Scribner's Sons, 1960), 566–570.

I discovered a long history connecting revivals and Presbyterian sacramental seasons, both in Scotland and in the United States. I found a considerable body of literature showing that much of the earlier revivalist tradition in New England and the Middle Atlantic states was also based on the eucharistic gatherings of Presbyterian and Independent Churches.

The immediate result of this discovery was that I understood the Stone side of my Christian Church heritage far better than I had previously. I developed a paper on this subject but made no effort to disseminate my findings until 1993 or 1994, when I presented the paper to my working group at the North American Academy of Liturgy. Although the other members of this group were also historians, none of them had known of this connection between evangelism and the Eucharist. The paper was subsequently published in *Discipliana*, the journal of the Disciples of Christ Historical Society.[63] By then, it was too late for my work to have much effect, because a book of major importance on this topic had already been published.[64] Nevertheless, I was pleased to have discovered this aspect of my eucharistic tradition that Disciples historians had somehow overlooked.

The question remains: Why is it that, despite our historic commitment to communion every Sunday, we Disciples seem to have so little interest in the theological implications of the Lord's supper in our movement? Even Newell Williams's 2000 biography of Barton W. Stone focuses less on the theological and spiritual aspects of the revival-sacrament connection than on the way the sacramental occasions entered into the organizational conflicts among Presbyterians in Kentucky and surrounding areas.[65] Soon thereafter I became aware of another extended monograph by a Disciples author on the theology of the Eucharist: Paul H. Jones's *Christ's Eucharistic Presence*.[66]

---

[63] Keith Watkins, "The Sacramental Character of the Camp Meeting," *Discipliana* 54, no. 1 (Spring 1994).

[64] Leigh Eric Schmidt, *Holy Fairs: Scottish Communions and American Revivals in the Early Modern Period* (Princeton, NY: Princeton University Press, 1989).

[65] Newell D. Williams, *Barton Stone: A Spiritual Biography* (St. Louis: Chalice Press, 2000).

[66] Paul H. Jones, *Christ's Eucharistic Presence: A History of the Doctrine* (New York: Peter Lang, 1994).

Toward a Disciples Book of Worship

Throughout my years at CTS, I occasionally heard the comment that someone needed to revise and reissue G. Edwin Osborn's *Christian Worship: A Service Book.* Even though it had long been out of print, it was the only serious effort since World War II to create a book of services and worship resources for Disciples. Claiming that Osborn had never sold well, the Disciples' publishing house, Christian Board of Publication, was not interested in bringing it out again. Even though I had used the book extensively in my early ministry, I had long since set it aside because the theology of worship, style of prayers, and liturgical forms were so out of step with the liturgical movement in which I was active. Yet, it was clear to me that Disciples needed to develop a book that could replace Osborn's. I was sure, however, that Disciples could not follow a method similar to the one used by most of the other churches. By the early 1980s, national church revenues had declined and there was not enough money to fund a liturgical commission. Furthermore, because Disciples were using the principle of representativeness as a more important criterion than scholarly background for appointing members of commissions, I doubted that we could put together a commission that would be able to create an adequate set of materials to distribute to our church.

I decided that both problems could be circumvented by developing an unofficial process using people from Indianapolis who could come together easily and inexpensively. Peter Morgan, the worship officer on the staff of Homeland Ministries, and Sherman Hanson, editor of our church press, supported the idea of convening a team of people related to Christian Theological Seminary. Michael Kinnamon had just come to our faculty upon the completion of a tour of service with the World Council of Churches in Geneva, where he had been closely associated with the Council's major new publication, *Baptism, Eucharist and Ministry*, which climaxed half a century of ecumenical work on these important topics.[67] Katherine Kinnamon was also experienced in liturgical matters, having coedited a collection of contemporary prayers from around the world.[68] Ronald Allen taught preaching and New Testament and

---

[67] Geneva, Switzerland: World Council of Churches, 1982.
[68] Katherine Kinnamon and Iben Gjerding (eds.), *No Longer Strangers: A Resource for Women and Worship* (Geneva, Switzerland: ATAR, 1982).

shared my interest in Susanne Langer's ideas. Linda McKiernan-Allen, an interim associate regional minister in Indiana, was well along in drafting a book on worship to be used in adult classes.[69] Peter Morgan, who met with us regularly, was especially interested in the Disciples' tradition of spirituality, which he had expressed in a book published early in our project.[70]

We were clear about the point of view our book would take: We would neither "prescribe how all worship should take place in Disciples of Christ congregations" nor simply "reinforce current Disciples practice." Instead, we would "take a strong stand about Disciples worship and its relationship to the universal church."[71] The book, which we titled *Thankful Praise*, was published in 1987 by Christian Board of Publication (along with a study guide written by J. Cy Rowell). It begins with a statement of principles, an outline for the Sunday service, and a commentary on the service. Most of *Thankful Praise* consists of scriptural materials, prayers, and other materials for worship, arranged according to the Christian year. One intention that guided our selection was that the book would stimulate discussion and creativity in congregations. Although we assumed the materials we published would be used in many places, we hoped that the tradition of extemporaneous prayer and locally developed materials would be strengthened by our publication.

At the Disciples' General Assembly following the publication of *Thankful Praise*, I presided over a workshop featuring the new "resource." Although many people responded enthusiastically to the book, some were sharply critical, criticizing the book's seeming diminishment of the responsibility of elders and strengthening of the pastoral role in the communion service. There was also strong opposition to the impression that we were advocating the use of standardized rather than extemporaneous prayers.

Soon thereafter, on behalf of the Disciples Division of Homeland Ministries, I convened a second team, with five contributors:

---

[69] Linda McKiernan-Allen, *We Worship in Spirit and in Truth* (St. Louis: Christian Board of Publication, 1988).

[70] Peter M. Morgan, *Story Weaving: Using Stories to Transform Your Congregation* (St. Louis: Christian Board of Publication, 1986).

[71] Keith Watkins (et. al.) *Thankful Praise: A Resource for Christian Worship* (St. Louis, MO: Christian Board of Publication, 1987), 8. C. J. Rowell, *Thankful Praise: A Study Guide* (St. Louis: Christian Board of Publication, 1987).

LaTaunya M. Bynum, Michael K. Kinnamon, Margaret A. Lowe, Peter M. Morgan, and Stephen B. Sprinkle. The book we developed, titled *Baptism and Belonging*, was published in 1991 and was a direct response to ecumenical discussions on the meaning and history of Christian baptism, with special emphasis on the renewed interest in adult baptism, which one Catholic scholar described as the theological norm of Christian worship. Three essays interpreted aspects of the ecumenical discussion. A study guide by William B. Rose-Heim was published in 1992.[72] I have no way of knowing the response of Disciples to these publications.

Although *Thankful Praise* was not widely reviewed or advertised, it came to the attention of Gerard Francis Moore, S.M., a graduate student in the School of Religious Studies at Catholic University of America. Two years after we published our book, Moore examined it in his dissertation, "The Eucharistic Theology of the Prayers for the Communion Service of the Lord's Supper of the Christian Church (Disciples of Christ): 1953–1987."[73] The first half of the dissertation reviewed the thinking of Alexander Campbell and other early Disciples leaders on the Lord's supper and described Disciples' worship books published in the late nineteenth century and the first decades of the twentieth. Moore gave more extended analysis of Osborn's *Christian Worship: A Service Book* and devoted the final third of the dissertation to an analysis and critique of *Thankful Praise* and the theology of the Eucharist that is expressed in its prayers.

This book's "most immediate achievement," Moore concluded, "is that it has placed Disciples worship firmly within the great tradition of Christian eucharistic worship." The communion prayers in Disciples congregations "had become narrow and introspective," and the order of worship in which it regularly appeared "was disjointed." In *Thankful Praise* "this isolation is broken and unity is restored to the service by the retrieval both of the relationship between Word and Sacrament and of the thanksgiving prayer over

---

[72] LaTaunya M. Bynum, Michael K. Kinnamon, Margaret A. Lowe, Peter M. Morgan, and Stephen B. Sprinkle (eds.), *Baptism and Belonging: A Resource for Christian Worship* (St. Louis: Chalice Press, 1991). William B. Rose-Heim, *Baptism and Belonging: A Study Guide* (St. Louis: Chalice Press, 1991).

[73] Gerard Francis Moore, "The Eucharistic Theology of the Prayers for the Communion Service of the Lord's Supper of the Christian Church (Disciples of Christ), 1953–1987." Unpublished dissertation (Washington, DC: The Catholic University of America, 1989).

loaf and cup which contains thanksgiving, *anamnesis, epiclesis,* and doxology."[74] The result, he wrote, is that "Disciples worship is greatly enriched and its ecumenical potential is broadened."[75] Moore noted the teaching potential in *Thankful Praise*, but he also recognized that the book "offers a host of challenges and theological insights to the Disciples."[76]

One of these challenges was a change of theological focus in communion prayers. The prevailing Disciples' emphasis had been on memorial, understood as recollection, and on Christ as Host at the table. In *Thankful Praise*, with its emphasis on *anamnesis* (remembrance) and *epiclesis* (calling on the Spirit), the prayers bring a new "approach to the question of 'real presence,'" which is more in line with *Baptism, Eucharist and Ministry*. Moore pointed out that *Thankful Praise* was inconsistent in that it contains prayers with both the older and newer ideas of remembrance. In what strikes me as a more difficult challenge, Moore suggested that these Disciples' prayers retained much of "the Reformation polemic, especially with regard to offering and sacrifice, and intercession." He summarized the way that ancient eucharistic prayers included these ideas and implied that Disciples' prayers would be much improved by recovering more of this ancient tradition. He also pointed to the book's inconsistency with respect to the themes of *epiclesis* and doxology, suggesting that this "deficiency" was caused by the inadequacy of models the authors used and by the Disciples' historic "neglect of the role of the Spirit at the Table."[77]

To my knowledge, Moore's dissertation is the only scholarly analysis of the Disciples' eucharistic tradition and practice. It reinforces objectives that have been central to my work both with Disciples and in the ecumenical circles where I have labored.

---

[74] These two words are from the Greek language that was widely used in the New Testament era, and they are used to refer to two parts of the eucharistic prayer. The *anamnesis*, which means the act of remembering, identifies the part of the prayer that specifically remembers Jesus Christ and the benefits of his life that are celebrated at the table. The *epiclesis*, which means the act of calling upon, refers to the part of the prayer that calls on the Holy Spirit. The Latin equivalent of this word gives us the English word *invocation*.

[75] Gerard Francis Moore, "The Eucharistic Theology of the Prayers," 142.

[76] Ibid., 144.

[77] Ibid., 147ff.

Although I appreciate the commendation that Moore gave to *Thankful Praise* and his more guarded support to the ecumenical contributions Disciples could make, I am even more attentive to his identification of the theological deficiency in these prayers. The team that created *Thankful Praise* was more committed to the historic traditions of eucharistic praying than most Disciples are likely to be. The ecumenical convergence on eucharistic praying is missing in the collection of meditations and prayers that Jane McAvoy gathered from more than thirty Disciples leaders even though the prayers represent a wide theological range and variety in length and form.[78] Eucharistic themes and a piety centered on the communion table are evident throughout the volume, yet the book as a whole illustrates Moore's critique of Disciples prayer at the table—it is narrow and introspective, separated from the "great tradition of Christian worship."[79]

For a quarter of a century, Moore's dissertation was available on a very limited basis, primarily in theological libraries. In 2015, however, Moore (using the name Gerard Moore, published a new popular edition entitled *The Disciples at the Lord's Table: Prayers Over Bread and Cup across 150 Years of Christian Church Worship.* In his preface, Moore expresses appreciation "to members of the Christian Church (Disciples of Christ) who have prodded me over the years about publishing the results of my research and my discussion of its implications." Including a comprehensive listing of books and essays on Disciples worship published through the years, this book is just over one hundred pages in length and gives the best listing of this material available today. In his closing reflection, Moore notes that "time, prayer, worship, and praxis will further determine the future of this way of Sunday worship, and mark its contribution to an ecumenical Christianity—so cherished an aim of Alexander Campbell and his followers."[80]

In 1997, a new comprehensive book of services and worship materials, titled *Chalice Worship*, was published for Disciples.

---

[78] Jane McAvoy, *Table Talk: Resources for the Communion Meal* (St. Louis: Chalice Press, 1993).

[79] Gerard Francis Moore, "The Eucharistic Theology of the Prayers," 142.

[80] Gerard Moore, *The Disciples at the Lord's Table: Prayers Over Bread and Cup across 150 Years of Christian Worship* (Eugene, OR: Pickwick Publications, 2015), 102.

Referring to *Thankful Praise*, the editors stated they had chosen "due to the limitations of space, not to replicate materials found in this most helpful book which is still in print."[81]

In recent times, I have realized that *Chalice Worship* was the culmination of an earlier process for developing a new Disciples worship book. It had begun during the 1940s, when the publishing houses of the American Baptist Convention and the Disciples of Christ published *Christian Worship: A Hymnal* for use in congregations of both communions. (Among the eight Disciples on the joint committee was William A. Shullenberger, for thirty-six years pastor of Central Christian Church in Indianapolis, where I am now a member.) Twenty years later, a new generation of American Baptist and Disciples decided to create a successor to the earlier book. Each church named fifteen members, including musicians and people knowledgeable in worship, to a hymnal committee to develop this new book. Because I taught worship at one of the Disciples' seminaries, I was one of our church's representatives and participated energetically. This was my first engagement in this kind of interdenominational activity. Although these meetings took place more than half a century ago, I still remember them as spirited and constructive. The new book, with the title *Hymnbook for Christian Worship*, was published in 1970. In addition to 454 hymns and other musical elements, the new hymnal contained 345 items in a section entitled "The Written Word." With respect to materials from the Bible and elsewhere that would be used in preparing Sunday worship, it could be used in much the same way as Osborn's *Christian Worship: A Service Book*.

In 1991, Disciples on their own appointed a fifteen-member hymnal development committee that began meeting, both in plenary and as two subcommittees: Language, Theology, and Worship; and Texts, Tunes, and Service Music. According to the preface, the committee members met fourteen times during a three-year period. They researched what congregations were then singing and the new explosion in church music, bringing together old hymns and new, and representing several ethnic traditions. The committee sought to "eliminate or reduce archaic language, generic masculine references for humanity, and the negative uses of metaphors about darkness or physical disabilities." In an interesting historical note, the editors

---

[81] Colbert S. Cartwright and O. I. Cricket Harrison (eds.), *Chalice Worship* (St. Louis: Chalice Press, 1997), xiii.

state that a "special feature of the hymnal is a three-year cycle of daily worship incorporating a psalm, a scripture text, and one of the hymns in this collection." They note that there "was a time when each Christian individual or family owned a personal hymnbook, for use as a devotional guide second in importance only to the Bible. *Chalice Hymnal* provides an opportunity for recovering that vital spiritual tradition."[82] With the name *Chalice Hymnal*, the new book was published in 1995.[83] Although I was not a member of the committee, I was well acquainted with four of the team, including Colbert S. Cartwright, who had served with me as Disciples' representatives on COCU's commission on worship.

When I joined him on that commission, Colbert was already well-known among Disciples. His father, Lin D. Cartwright, served as editorial secretary of the Christian Board of Publication. Among his books were *Evangelism Today* and *The Great Commitment: The Meaning of the Confession of Faith. "Do You Believe with All Your Heart that Jesus is the Christ."*[84] According to the biographical sketch on one of his books, Colbert Cartwright had held pastorates in "tradition-rich Lynchburg, racially-troubled Little Rock, steel-centered Youngstown, and Disciples-steeped Fort Worth." He then became area minister of the Trinity-Brazos Area of the Christian Church in the Southwest. His two books—*People of the Chalice: Disciples of Christ in Faith and Practice* (1987) and *Candles of Grace: Disciples Worship in Perspective* (1992)— demonstrate his deep understanding of the Disciples and his skill as a writer.

Joining him as an editor of *Chalice Worship* was a much younger writer named O. I. Cricket Harrison who, after serving as a Disciples pastor, taught worship and church music at Lexington Theological Seminary and served on the development committee for *Chalice Hymnal* and *Chalice Praise*. In "A Coda to the Introduction," Harrison refers to the fragile character of Colbert's health and noted that, even so, he had completed his work on the development committees for *Chalice Hymnal*, the *Chalice Hymnal Worship Leader's Guide*, and *Chalice Worship* before he died. She also names David P. Polk, editor

---

[82] Chalice Editors, *Chalice Hymnal* (St. Louis, MO: Chalice Press, 1995), vi.

[83] The Disciples' publishing house had by now adopted the title "Chalice Press."

[84] Ibid., 770, 774

of Chalice Press, as "truly the unnamed third editor" of *Chalice Worship.*[85]

Clearly, Colbert brought his extensive knowledge of ecumenical discussions about worship to his work as chair of language, theology, and worship. Especially interesting to me are two orders for the eucharistic service: "An Order for the Lord's Supper with Those Confined" and "Basic Resources for Sunday Worship." Included are examples of prayers at the table. My impression is that *Chalice Hymnal* is used in most English-speaking Disciples congregations across the United States and Canada.

Chalice Worship, a full book of services and prayers, the Disciples' counterpart to similar volumes published by other churches, including the United Church of Christ, the Evangelical Lutheran Church, and The Church of the Province of New Zealand. It begins by presenting a set of "general services of worship," two of which are outlines for the regular Sunday morning service of word and sacrament. The ecumenical impact on Disciples is evident in that both outlines follow the order that is standard in almost all churches of Christendom, except those of the Christian Church tradition. One of the two is taken from *Thankful Praise.*[86] Later, *Chalice Worship* included the full "Service for the Sacrament of the Lord's Supper" published by the Consultation on Church Union.[87]

One of the significant advances in *Chalice Worship* is that it provides instructions and illustrative texts for use at the communion table, including the actual content and form of communion prayers. While acknowledging that "there is a diversity of views as to what shape the communion prayers should take within Disciples congregations," the editors identify three elements that are central to these prayers: thanking God for creation, remembering God's acts of salvation in Jesus Christ, and calling on the Holy Spirit to draw the people into the presence of the risen Christ. Fourteen prayers are offered that "reflect the diversity of practices among present-day Disciples."[88] The comprehensiveness of *Chalice Worship* makes it a genuine successor to *Christian Worship: A Service Book*. Although its theological presuppositions, literary style, and liturgical contents

---

[85] Cartwright and Harrison, *Chalice Worship*, xiii.
[86] Ibid., 10–14.
[87] Ibid., 79–84.
[88] Ibid., 408–409.

differ significantly from its predecessor, the book continues to be very much a Disciples' book. What G. Edwin Osborn had said nearly half a century earlier could also be said of this new volume: It reflects what Disciples already are doing rather well and is not an effort to force new ways upon a reluctant church. One Disciples pastor concluded his careful review of *Chalice Worship* with the observation—perhaps too critical—that it represents much movement but little progress.[89]

This new Disciples' worship book is the only one published by a recognized unit of our church to acknowledge the importance of the ecumenical consensus concerning worship. No other Disciples' publication with which I am familiar attempts to connect our liturgical practice to the broad eucharistic tradition that has transformed Christianity during the last half century.

The Eucharist as Norm for Christian Worship

Another way to describe what has happened is to say that Disciples have experienced much the same process as have other churches in the modern liturgical movement. The hard work of scholars, pastors, and other leaders in the field of worship has brought the churches much closer to one another than they have ever been before. Yet the distinctive character of each liturgical tradition has been confirmed and each of the historic Western churches has settled back into a mode of worship that expresses many of its long-standing patterns and practices.

My many years in the classroom had already alerted me to the conservatism of the churches concerning worship on Sunday mornings. I taught my basic course nearly fifty times, always emphasizing the classic tradition that is the foundation upon which most churches base their worship. I always emphasized the eucharistic norm of Christian worship, but I organized the course so that students were to bring their own experiences in worship into conversation with this classic tradition. Many of my students responded enthusiastically to this approach; yet many others resisted the emphasis on the classic service of word and table. They were largely indifferent to the convergence among the churches,

---

[89] Douglas Dornhecker, "Chalice Worship: How Goes the Reformation?" Paper presented to Northwest Association for Theological Discussion, February 3–5, 1998.

almost always reaffirming their commitment to the patterns of worship that were traditional in their respective faith communities.

After 1987, when the seminary moved into the new Sweeney Chapel, we developed a weekly pattern of worship that included the Eucharist one day a week in the official schedule and a brief service early in the morning as part of the unofficial schedule. On most occasions we used an order that was consistent with the skeleton in the new worship books and compact prayers that were newly composed for the occasion. Attendance was strong in the official service, and the liturgy, which was specific to Sweeney Chapel, enabled people of various liturgical families to worship together. Nearly all in the congregation, and especially Disciples, however, maintained a strong sense of loyalty to their own ways of eucharistic celebration.

The strongest sign of the liturgical convergence during the years I was teaching is the shelf of worship books that were published during the last quarter of the twentieth century, beginning with *The Lutheran Book of Worship* in 1978 and concluding with the Presbyterian *Book of Common Worship* in 1993. The eucharistic liturgies in these books are very much alike in shape, style, tone, and theology. Although they allow individual adaptation in ceremony and language, they can be described as several variations of the same rite. Perhaps it would be more accurate to say that there are two variations of the eucharistic rite in these churches—the modified Mass and the post-Reformation service of word and table. Examples of the modified Mass are the post-Vatican Roman rite, the Lutheran service of holy communion, and the Episcopal liturgy of the holy Eucharist. There are three variants of the Reformed service—Methodist, United Church of Christ, and Presbyterian. Disciples' services of the Lord's supper, published in *Chalice Worship*, also are based on the post-Reformation pattern, but prevailing practice in most Disciples congregations shows relatively little connection to historic Protestant antecedents.

In most congregations of the historic Western churches, the Eucharist is celebrated more frequently than had previously been the practice. The two exceptions are the Roman Catholic Church and the Disciples, as both of these communions have always considered the Eucharist as integral to the regular worship of their congregations. Yet the principal service on most Sundays in Lutheran, Presbyterian,

Methodist, and United Church of Christ congregations continues to be a service of the word rather than the Eucharist. After developing strong, new eucharistic liturgies, these churches have settled into a largely non-eucharistic equilibrium, each of them reasserting its traditional character. Although the Roman Catholic Church has made radical changes in the language and style of its worship, one thing has not changed. The center of gravity of its worship—or one might say the commanding metaphor—continues to be the altar. Modern reforms have restored preaching, prayers, and praise to places of prominence, but the Eucharist continues to be the driving power of Roman Catholic worship. The primary change is that this focal point of the Mass is understood as a table, so that the communal character of the action is highlighted. This development is consistent with the Catholic Church's historic identification with the people, embracing many kinds and conditions and bringing them fully into the church's liturgical life. That power has been increased by the post-Vatican adoption of the vernacular in worship and renewal of the Mass so that it serves as the people's prayer.

Four of the traditions—Lutheran, Presbyterian, Methodist, and United Church of Christ—have strengthened the role of the Eucharist in their worship but continue to give higher priority to services of the word. In this regard, they are faithful to their sixteenth-century heritage, in which the word of God replaced the sacrament of the altar as the controlling metaphor of the church's life. Whatever Luther may have intended, the church tradition that bears his name quickly became word-centered, even though a strong attachment to the Eucharist continued. Calvin gave less attention to maintaining the balance than Luther had done, and his spiritual descendants have always been word-centered. I first realized the continuing dominance of the word over the altar, even in writers who give much attention to the Eucharist, when I was working my way through Geoffrey Wainwright's highly acclaimed book *Doxology*.[90] It became clear to me that, despite his long interest in the Eucharist and his intense collaboration with leaders of the ecumenical movement, Wainwright was developing his theology of the Eucharist out of his theology of proclamation. As a Methodist, he had been shaped so fully by the metaphor of the word that it continued to control his work.

---

[90] Geoffrey Wainwright, *Doxology: The Praise of God in Worship, Doctrine, and Life* (New York: Oxford University Press, 1980).

The Christian Church tradition is an anomaly. From its earliest days, its congregations have maintained the every-Lord's Day Lord's supper; and the piety of the people in these churches is devotionally centered on the table. Even so, Disciples are authentic children of the sixteenth-century Reformation and therefore our controlling metaphor is more word of God than the sacrament of the table. In a paper developed for the first Disciples Study Commission, Harry Baker Adams suggested that the Disciples' "lack of interest in the liturgical developments in the church through its history" could be explained by their "emphasis on the worship of the New Testament Church." Changes in worship were understood as apostasy, and Disciples have "proposed to leap over the centuries to return to the 'purity' of the New Testament practices."[91] Today that commitment to restoring New Testament practice has waned among Disciples and, along with others in the post-Reformation tradition, their sense of biblical authority is attenuated. Even with this weakening of the word as center of gravity, the table has not become more prominent. Instead, it too has diminished, with the result that Disciples cling to their existing practices, scarcely changed by their contacts with other churches in the ecumenical movement.

One church among ecumenical Protestant denominations that has experienced significant development during this period of liturgical renewal is the Episcopal Church. When I began my teaching, the common pattern in Episcopal churches was to celebrate the Eucharist in an early service and to use the liturgy of morning prayer with sermon as the major service most Sundays. Although historians and liturgical scholars claimed that the intention in the original prayer book was for the Eucharist to be the primary service, this practice was maintained in only some of the parish churches. By the time the 1979 *Book of Common Prayer* was approved for use, this pattern had changed. In virtually all Episcopal parishes across the country, the Eucharist had become the principal liturgy for most the Sunday services. For much of its history, the Episcopal Church had struggled over the form and content of the eucharistic prayer. The texts provided in the 1979 prayer book resolved these problems. Perhaps most important of the changes is that the Episcopal Church has reached consensus concerning the central doctrines of the

---

[91] Harry Baker Adams, "Worship Among Disciples of Christ, 1865–1920," *Mid-Stream* 7, no. 4 (Summer 1968), 42.

Eucharist—Christ's real presence and the eucharistic sacrifice. The long-standing debates between the Anglo-Catholic and low-church portions of the church have been transcended, so that the conflicts have largely disappeared.[92] The Episcopal Church's involvement in the ecumenical movement has resulted in the completion of the liturgical reforms that had begun 400 years earlier and for many reasons had been frustrated over the generations. It has been decisively demonstrated that for Episcopalians the controlling metaphor for worship is the altar rather than the word.

Toward the close of my teaching career, I wrote a book that expresses much of what I had been teaching in my classes for a generation. Its title indicates the conviction that has marked my work: *The Great Thanksgiving: The Eucharistic Norm of Christian Worship*.[93] The book uses the third chapter of the New Testament book of Colossians as the key to understanding the early liturgical tradition, stating that Christian worship began as a special kind of thanksgiving for God's redemptive work in and through Jesus Christ. It shows how this motif shaped Christian worship throughout most of its history. I refer to an essay from the early 1960s, "The Norm and Freedom of Christian Worship," in which theologian Frederick Hertzog asserts that the purpose of Christian worship is to enable the congregation "to grasp the crude shape of what God has done in Christ." The church, he says, is free to use any liturgical means to accomplish that purpose, but it is inconceivable that the church would forego the use of the service of bread and wine as its primary means to do so.[94]

Nearly sixty years have passed since then, and Hertzog's statement holds true for churches of the catholic traditions—Orthodox, Roman Catholic, and Anglican—and, to a lesser degree, for the Christian Church movement. Mainline Protestant churches, however, depend more on the word than on the Eucharist, and Pentecostal and charismatic churches, many of which are growing rapidly, depend on spirited music, salvation-oriented preaching, and

---

[92] Byron D. Stuhlman, *Eucharistic Celebration, 1789–1979* (New York: Church Hymnal Corporation, 1988), 159ff.

[93] Keith Watkins, *The Great Thanksgiving: The Eucharistic Norm of Christian Worship* (St. Louis: Chalice Press, 1995).

[94] Frederick Hertzog, "The Norm and Freedom of Christian Worship." In Massey H. Shepherd, Jr. (ed.), *Worship in Scripture and Tradition* (New York: Oxford University Press, 1963), 118ff.

ecstatic experience as their major modes of connecting worshipers to God's saving work in Jesus Christ.

Despite this surge among non-eucharistic churches, my convictions concerning the eucharistic norm remain intact, and my worshiping life will continue to take place in churches that celebrate the Lord's supper as their regular Sunday mode of worship. Of course, the most frequent locale will be congregations of the Christian Church (Disciples of Christ), because this church family continues to be my personal and professional home. I know the history of this church body, understand its liturgical traditions and practices, and am supported in my Christian life by worship in its congregations. I appreciate the fact that my church has maintained the celebration of the Lord's supper as one aspect of popular Protestantism.

Three

Churches in Covenant Communion

Early in my years at the Multnomah Church of Christ, I learned one of the distinguishing ideas of the Christian Church movement: that the divided state of the church is wrong and that our churches have a plan that will bring about Christian unity. The restoration plea, as we called this plan, consisted of a few easily stated ideas that made sense to me when I heard them. The most important of these ideas was that the basic characteristics of the one church that God intends are presented in the New Testament, either in explicit command or in clear precedents. All people who studied the Bible in a serious and systematic way would come to essentially the same conclusions about these characteristics. Division in the church resulted when people replaced these scriptural characteristics with their own humanly devised ideas and practices. Unity would be achieved when people set aside these human opinions and practices and restored the main characteristics of the church of the New Testament era.

The congregations of the Christian Church movement, I was taught, had already reestablished these New Testament features: believers' baptism by immersion for the remission of sins, communion every Sunday, elder-led ministry, extemporaneous praying, and congregational government. Other churches were invited to reform their own practices in keeping with the simple forms of New Testament Christianity, and the result would be Christian unity.

I learned this line of thought well, as it was taught by our pastor and elders, expounded in study books that we used in church, and explained in church camps and retreats I attended. I had virtually no experience in any other church, nor was I familiar with the ideas and practices of other churches, especially those in the liturgical traditions. Therefore, I had no independent way of discerning what might have been early Christian practices.

These ideas were confirmed at Northwest Christian College, where I enrolled immediately after graduation from high school. All of the faculty and most of the students were active members of the Christian Church movement. We came to the college because of our commitment to the restoration plea and our intention of becoming active leaders of the churches that shared this commitment. The people on campus, however, were divided into two groups—Cooperatives and Independents—who held this plea in somewhat different modes.

The point of contention was their support or nonsupport of the Indianapolis- and St. Louis-based agencies and offices that had emerged among the more liberal congregations of the movement. Cooperative churches, such as First Christian Church in Portland, supported these agencies and held a moderate to liberal theological position. Independent churches (which also were referred to as direct-support congregations), such as Multnomah Church of Christ, refused to support these agencies and, instead, supported programs and colleges that depended primarily on one congregation or a small group of congregations for their financial undergirding. These congregations tended toward traditional theological understandings of the Bible.

Whereas in much of the United States, Cooperatives and Independents had already drifted apart so that they were virtually separate networks, in Oregon and at Northwest Christian College, the two groups maintained a fairly extensive pattern of interaction. Church people were loath to acknowledge that their unity movement had broken into two factions, and some semblance of unity stayed in place. We still believed that our Christian Church approach to Christian unity was correct and would, in time, be effective.

Although the two factions were named (we could say "denominated") because of disputes over organizations beyond the congregation, a more important cause of division was the relation of baptism to church membership. The traditional understanding of baptism in the churches of the Christian Church movement was that candidates for this ordinance of the church had to be old enough to believe the gospel and publicly affirm that faith. They would then be baptized in the name of the Father, Son, and Holy Spirit, by full immersion in water. Only people baptized this way could be accepted into membership in a congregation.

Most people in the Christian Church movement acknowledged that people baptized some other way—which usually meant during infancy by sprinkling—could be considered Christians and thereby welcomed to participate in church activities, including receiving communion week after week. Yet they could not become members of a congregation until they "completed their obedience to the Lord," which was the language we used to describe their being baptized by full immersion. Congregations that adhered to the traditional practice were described as closed membership churches, whereas congregations that would accept "the pious unimmersed" into full membership without being immersed were described as open membership churches. Across the country a growing number of congregations had become open membership churches. In Oregon, however, most congregations adhered to the traditional practice.

There was no doubt in my mind concerning the correctness of the traditional understanding of baptism and its relation to church membership. I was firmly committed to a closed membership position. The difficulty of this conviction came to me forcefully in evangelistic calls that I made as a student minister of the Christian Church in Dayton, Oregon. Although I was engaged in these conversations several times, the one I remember clearly was with a Lutheran couple who attended our church regularly. Because there was no Lutheran church in our community, they had chosen the Christian Church as the one in which to be active; they would gladly have become members, except for the requirement that members had to be immersed. They insisted that the baptism by sprinkling they had received as infants in the Lutheran Church was real baptism and that they were real Christians. They asked why our church received them so completely and why we would allow them to receive communion if we doubted the authenticity of their standing as Christians. We were requiring that they impugn what God had done for them and submit to rebaptism. Nothing that I could say, including the standard Disciples' response that what we required was not rebaptism but the completion of their obedience, could overcome their theological rejection of our church's requirement. They countered by saying that if they should decide to submit to this requirement, it would be solely because they had to do it in order to be members of this congregation. They would continue to think of their baptism in the Lutheran Church as their real baptism.

Even then I could see the contradiction in my church's position. If baptism, defined as the immersion of penitent believers, was the entrance into the Christian life, then people baptized in some other way were not Christian. People in the Christian Church movement had shied away from this conclusion, however, because of the fact that there were so many Methodists, Lutherans, Baptists, Presbyterians, and even Roman Catholics who believed in Jesus Christ, attended church faithfully, and lived lives that were fully Christian. How could we deny the Christian status of people who so obviously were Christian? Yet, if we were to acknowledge that these people were Christians despite the fact that their baptism was so different from the baptism our churches insisted on, then we had little basis on which to deny them full participation in the membership and life of our congregations.

This conundrum was partially solved for me by a comment that I heard one day in a conversation on campus at Northwest Christian College. A group of students was discussing this very matter with Professor Lawrence Bixler, a highly regarded member of the faculty who defended the traditional ideas and practices of the Christian Church movement. One of the students had asked if people who had been baptized as infants were really Christians. Bixler's vigorous response was, "Of course, they're Christian even though their baptism is irregular." Although I wasn't sure what to do next, I was convinced on the spot that my Lutheran congregants were Christians with full rights to membership in the congregation. While I would continue to teach the "regular" pattern of baptism—the immersion of penitent believers—I would have to find a better way of dealing with people who had been baptized in a different way.

Moving into the Disciples Mainstream

As my college graduation approached, I, along with nearly half of my seminary-bound classmates, applied for admission to the bachelor of divinity program at the Butler School of Religion. Although the School of Religion was as much a part of the Christian Church movement as was Northwest Christian College, the Cooperative-Independent relationship was significantly different. In contrast to the Oregon campus, where Cooperatives and Independents tried to live as though there was no rift, the Indianapolis campus accepted the fact that these two groups stood on opposite sides of a crevasse that seemed to be growing wider and deeper. The seminary required that Christian Church applicants declare whether they were Cooperative or Independent, so that their placement as student ministers could be made in congregations sympathetic to their point of view. I had concluded—for reasons that I no longer remember—to register as a Cooperative, despite the fact that all of my previous experience had been in Independent churches.

I was invited to consider the Christian Church in Somerset, Indiana, which had been severely conflicted with their most recent pastor, who was a highly partisan Independent. Robert Lewis, the placement officer, assured me that the people were "Cooperative at heart." What I discovered was a traditional Christian Church in which the Cooperative–Independent divide didn't matter. The congregation historically had supported agencies that were connected to the Cooperative side of things, including the Emily Flynn Home in nearby Marion, Indiana; it also supported a youth camp and other activities that were connected to the Independent side. The church practiced closed membership, as it had always done, but it also participated fully in inter-church activities in its community. Longtime members knew why they were Disciples rather than Methodists, yet they readily affirmed that friends and family members in these other churches were really Christians.

My confidence in the Christian Church approach to achieving unity was tested by experiences with other ministers in the Somerset community. Although we were some ten miles out in the country, we were considered members of the ministerial association in our county-seat town of Wabash. At a breakfast meeting, several of us were comparing the origins of our communions. I gave the standard reason for my church—that we came into being in order to reestablish the central features of the church revealed in the New Testament. To my consternation, my Methodist and Brethren conversation partners declared that their churches had been created for that same reason. All three of us claimed to be New Testament churches, yet we differed significantly from one another in our modes of baptism, worship, and ministry, and in our polities and relationships to culture.

My perplexity deepened as I read a book loaned to me by the pastor of a Brethren church with whom I felt a strong kinship. It was a vigorous exposition of the distinctive characteristics of his church, closely parallel in form to books about the Christian Churches that I had read during my youth at the Multnomah Church of Christ. The books I read in earlier years had demonstrated the superiority of our practice of baptism by means of a table that headed the vertical columns with passages of scripture describing baptism and designated the horizontal rows with the three modes of baptism. The only mode of baptism that earned a check mark under all the scripture passages was immersion of believers. Sprinkling, pouring, and infant baptism all had blanks in some of the columns. The conclusion was that the one mode of baptism with checks in all the columns was the only one in which all Christians could be secure.

The Brethren book, to my surprise, had the same kind of table, but it included an additional column and a fourth form of baptism that my Christian Church book did not have: triple immersion. The one form of baptism with checks in all of the columns was triple immersion, and my church's single immersion was shown to be deficient. If I were to be faithful to the logic that previously had been so persuasive to me, I would have to have completed my own obedience by being immersed two more times.

The anomaly was increased when my friend told me that he could easily affirm that I was a Christian and a minister. He could invite me to be guest preacher at his church. Yet he could not invite me to participate in the celebration of the Lord's supper and the foot-washing ceremony that preceded it because my baptism did not conform to the biblical standard. To settle the dissonance that had been created, I had to find out which of the two forms of baptism—single or triple immersion—was the form used by churches in the New Testament. I asked my professor, William Robinson, if triple (sometimes called trine) immersion could have been the practice of the early church. He reassured me with his immediate response that the trine-immersion tradition had neither biblical warrant nor precedent in the apostolic and post-apostolic church. Although relieved at his response, I was still uneasy about this matter. Furthermore, I was confident that if it would be shown that

New Testament baptism really was triple immersion, the Christian Churches would nevertheless hold fast to their practice of single immersion. We, like my Lutheran congregants, would insist that our first baptism was full and complete. We, too, would resist the idea that we should complete our obedience by a double rebaptism.

Later, when I looked into the history myself, I found an article in an encyclopedia claiming that the original form of baptism may have been the triple application of water, perhaps by drenching a person with water poured over head and shoulders. While my confidence in the form of baptism in my church was being tested, I was reassured by William Robinson's writings that believers were the proper recipients of baptism. In his book *What Churches of Christ Stand For*, first published in 1926, Robinson stated that "the greatest contribution Churches of Christ have made to religious thought" is the doctrine of conversion. Tied up as it is with the doctrine of baptism, the doctrine of conversion is what divides Churches of Christ from "all other organized Christian bodies." Their understanding is close to the doctrine of baptism "which has been accepted in the Catholic Church from the earliest ages"—that it is for the remission of sins. Churches of Christ agree that faith and repentance are prerequisites for baptism, "but they do not allow that faith and repentance can be exercised by proxy," which means they reject infant baptism.[1]

While I was thinking about the baptism–membership issues that threatened the unity of the Christian Church movement, I was also considering the institutional separation that was taking place. One of my reasons for choosing the School of Religion as my seminary was its location in Indianapolis, where several of the national agencies of the Christian Churches were located. I anticipated that it would be possible to become personally acquainted with the mission boards and other organizations, along with their leaders, and thus be better able to make a long-term decision concerning my ministry. I soon discovered that by living and studying in Indiana, I also could become better acquainted with the independent agencies and leaders. Midway through my B.D. studies, the North American Christian Convention met at Cadle Tabernacle, at that time an important

---

[1] William Robinson, *What Churches of Christ Stand For* (Birmingham, UK: The Berean Press, 1946), 55–56. *Churches of Christ* is the name by which Disciples were known in Great Britain.

center for religious convocations in Indianapolis. In the exhibit hall, I discovered that the Independents also had a full array of colleges, mission organizations, and other church agencies.

I could see two differences between the organizations that exhibited at the North American Christian Convention and those that exhibited at the International Convention of the Disciples of Christ. Whereas the Disciples agencies enjoyed a national constituency, the North American organizations, for the most part, were freelance or related to only a few congregations. Even Bible colleges, which were coming into existence all around the country, tended to be sponsored by small regional clusters of congregations. The second difference was in the character of these institutions. How could Lincoln Bible College be compared with Bethany College or Texas Christian University, or any of the direct-support mission programs with the United Christian Missionary Society? I could see that, as a pastor, I and any congregation I would serve would necessarily participate in a network of other pastors, congregations, and organizations beyond the congregation. It made little sense to try to participate in two parallel systems, as would be necessary if one tried to maintain the Oregon pattern of Cooperative-Independent relations. Thus, the question was which of the parallel networks would I choose as the one in which I would work.

The decision I was making in the exhibit hall was confirmed by the keynote address, delivered by the convention president, James G. Van Buren, a pastor from Pittsburgh. His sermon dealt with the challenges that the Independent Christian Churches were facing as they tried to work for Christian unity according to the principles of the restoration plea. He acknowledged that relations within the Christian Church movement often were hostile, and he defended the attitudes of Independents toward Cooperatives with a wartime analogy: When you take prisoners from your enemy's forces, you treat them humanely according to the Geneva Convention. When you capture your own forces engaged in treason, you shoot them at sunrise. I was astonished and angered by his harsh ideas and bombastic manner. I could not imagine committing myself to working for a lifetime in an enterprise with that spirit in one of its most prominent leaders.

The decisions that were taking shape that evening at Cadle Tabernacle were confirmed by my experiences with leaders of the Cooperative churches. The most sustained contact was in a conference for seminary seniors, presented by the major Disciples agencies, in which the senior officers briefed us on the work of their organizations.[2] The people who stood out were A. Dale Fiers, president of the United Christian Missionary Society; Virgil Sly, executive secretary of the foreign division of the United Society; and Harley L. Smith, president of the Board of Higher Education. Fiers had been a pastor most of his ministry and Sly a mission executive. Smith was not a minister and, prior to coming to his current position, had been the president of a Disciples college. Individually and as a group, these men came across as principled, effective, mature leaders of the church. I looked forward to working in a network led by people of their maturity and Christian character.

The B.D. program at the School of Religion required a thesis, and I decided that this requirement provided me the opportunity to make sense out of the Disciples' vocation of Christian unity. With Professor Ronald E. Osborn as my advisor, I wrote my one-hundred-page paper with the title, "Disciples of Christ in Ecumenical Encounter." The five chapter headings indicate the scope of the thesis: early development of the Disciples' position, ecumenical encounter on the doctrinal level, ecumenical encounter on the institutional level, internal reactions to the ecumenical encounter, and basic problems of the Disciples revealed by their ecumenical encounter. I read a wide range of Disciples authors, beginning with Thomas Campbell, Alexander Campbell, and Barton W. Stone, and concluding with my own teachers, William Robinson, Ronald E. Osborn, and William J. Richardson. The thesis could be considered an exercise in applied ecclesiology, because it was primarily institutional and secondarily theological, dealing with the restoration plea as a methodology for relating to the wider Christian world rather than as a coherent theological exposition of the nature of the church and the meaning of the sacraments and the ministry.

Although the first four chapters presented the history of the ecumenical encounter of the Christian Church movement, the final chapter was the one in which I presented my questions and

---

[2] This conference was the first in a series that continued many years thereafter. Early in the process, however, the invitations were extended to seminary "middlers," students midway through their B.D. programs, rather than to seniors.

conclusions about my ecclesial tradition. It was clear to me that the ecumenical movement was requiring that all churches reappraise "their own existence and position." This necessity was even greater for Disciples, because of their advocacy of Christian unity. "Ultimately," I declared, the Disciples' "contribution to the united church, and immediately, their meaningful existence as a separate body will depend upon how seriously they study themselves, and how honestly they meet the problems revealed by their study."[3]

The section of this final chapter that was most important to me as the writer was the conclusion that contradicted the position of Professor Richardson. The mild tone of the thesis at this point belies the emotion I felt. Until writing this thesis, I had been persuaded by one of Richardson's lectures in which he asserted that denominationalism was characterized by emphasizing human innovations rather than "the common ground of the faith." His conclusion confirmed ideas I had learned at the Multnomah Church of Christ and Northwest Christian College: Disciples cannot be called a denomination because none of the opinions or methods in our churches "change the character of the Christian religion," nor are they made "a test of fellowship."[4]

Although I was still inclined to agree with Richardson that Disciples did not emphasize the things that distinguished us from others, my reading and reflection led me to the conclusion that his definition of denominationalism was inadequate. Instead, I was persuaded by the definition given by C. C. Morrison who, because of his editorship of the *Christian Century* was a Disciple known beyond our own ecclesial boundaries. In his book *The Unfinished Reformation*, Morrison defined a denomination as "a part of the Church of Christ existing in a structure of its own and exercising by itself and for itself those functions which belong to the unity of the whole Church of Christ."[5] I cited other Disciples authors, including Ronald E. Osborn, who also asserted that Disciples had become a

---

[3] Keith Watkins, "Disciples of Christ in Ecumenical Encounter" (B.D. thesis, Butler University, 1956), 73.

[4] William J. Richardson, "Toward Christian Unity: Addresses Given at the Oregon Christian Missionary Convention, 1951," 8. The quotation appears on page 75 of my thesis.

[5] C. C. Morrison, *The Unfinished Reformation* (New York: Harper & Brothers, 1953), 56. Quoted in Keith Watkins, "Disciples of Christ in Ecumenical Encounter," 76.

denomination. My break with Richardson—and with the central claims of the Christian Church movement as I had held them until then—was made complete when I realized that I agreed with another Disciples leader, George Stuart, who was writing in response to the Evanston, Illinois, assembly of the World Council of Churches. Stuart declared that Disciples had "developed a theology, a polity and identifiable doctrines" that, while not uniform among us, were "reflected in the divisions which undeniably exist among us. To deny our responsibilities as a church is the essence of sectarianism."[6]

By this time, I had become convinced that Disciples were not what we thought ourselves to be—the full and complete expression of the church as Jesus and the apostles intended it. I now knew that the other churches would not give up their own traditions and practices and become just like the Disciples. I realized that my previous understanding of Christian unity was naïve and that a much different approach would need to be taken. What had become a more persuasive way of framing the unity issue was an idea expressed with two sets of contrasting characteristics: The church is eschatological and historical, and it is spiritual and institutional. In its eschatological and spiritual sense, the church is one. Historically and institutionally, it is divided. The task for Christians at any point in history is to establish "a dialogue with others within an eschatological unity in the search for historical unity with them." It is to give "institutional expression to our spiritual unity."[7]

Fortunately, I found an exemplar of the dialogue in which Disciples needed to participate: my professor, William Robinson. Although he insisted on the authority of the New Testament, his understanding was more dynamic than I had encountered previously, for he believed that scripture allows the possibility of development "in harmony with the principles found in the New Testament." Furthermore, there are ambiguities on some matters

---

[6] George Stuart, "The Disciples and Evanston," *The Christian-Evangelist* (March 10, 1954), 223. Quoted in Watkins, "Disciples of Christ in Ecumenical Encounter," 77–78. At the time he wrote, Stuart was a pastor in Illinois. Shortly thereafter, he was appointed to the faculty of Christian Theological Seminary.

[7] The first quotation is from William Nichols, *Ecumenism and Catholicity* (London, UK: S.C.M. Press, 1952), 57–58; the second is from Ronald E. Osborn, "Disciples & Union Among Denominations," *Shane Quarterly* 16 (1955), 110, both cited in Keith Watkins, "Disciples of Christ in Ecumenical Encounter," 79.

described in the New Testament that require interpretation. Robinson stated that the church is "an organism that must grow, but it must never grow out of itself into something else."[8] Although these ideas were decidedly contrary to those with which I had grown up, Robinson also spoke of matters that were more consistent with traditional Christian Church positions: the "marks of the church—the one Faith, the ordinances of Baptism and the Lord's Supper, and the divinely appointed ministry."[9] His elaboration of these marks showed both his Disciples convictions and his full engagement in discussion with people in other church traditions. Although I had yet to grasp the import of Robinson's point of view, he provided a way for me to change the direction in which I would do theology. Instead of looking back to the Campbells and Stone, I would look forward toward a new definition of Christian unity and new patterns for the life of the church.

In the closing pages of my thesis, I asked how Disciples could justify their continuing existence and gave answers that were representative of the views that prominent church leaders were giving. It now seems clear, from the way I organized the last pages of the thesis, that I largely agreed with Ronald E. Osborn and Virgil Sly, both of whom believed that if Disciples continued the way they were, they would find themselves "remaining in the status of a small, aloof sect in a world where denominations are drawing together."[10] My hope, as was Osborn's, was that Disciples would awaken from their theological slumbers and move once again into the mainstream of theological discussion about the church and related issues.

The immediate and practical conclusion to my reflections at the School of Religion was that I would do my ministry within the Cooperative framework. My call to the pastorate of First Christian Church of Sanger, California, was the result. The transition from my Independent upbringing, however, was easily accomplished, as the Sanger congregation was closed membership and traditional

---

[8] William Robinson, *Essays on Christian Unity* (London, UK: James Clarke and Co., 1922), 162ff., cited in Watkins, "Disciples of Christ in Ecumenical Encounter," 86.

[9] William Robinson, *What Churches of Christ Stand For*, 74–75.

[10] Ronald E. Osborn, "Problems of Disciple Participation in the Ecumenical Movement," *Shane Quarterly* 15 (1954), 16–20, cited in Watkins, "Disciples of Christ in Ecumenical Encounter," 91.

in its ideas and practices. During the third and last year of my service at this church, I encountered the baptism-membership issue in a direct pastoral way—in a membership class for young adults who were attending our church. One woman had grown up in this congregation and been baptized in her pre-adolescent years. As an adult, she had moved to another community, married, and joined a Methodist church. She could rejoin First Christian Church in Sanger by simple transfer of membership. Her husband had been baptized by sprinkling as an infant in a Methodist church but had been nonobservant in his adult life. He was now ready to become an active member of our congregation but would have to be rebaptized by immersion. Another man had grown up with little church connection but during college years had been converted in the Episcopal Church's campus ministry and had been baptized by sprinkling. Even though he had been baptized as a believer, he would have to be rebaptized by immersion in order to transfer membership to our congregation. His wife had never been a Christian and would make her confession of faith and be baptized by immersion.

I explained the situation with an idea that I had heard Ronald E. Osborn use in connection with open and closed communion: that we have inherited a historical situation that we don't like and can't change. As pastor of a closed-membership church, I told them, I had to adhere to the congregation's membership policy even though I no longer could affirm it myself. All four of these people, along with others in the class, were willing to accept this explanation and take the appropriate action.

I concluded, however, that I would no longer take responsibility for interpreting the congregation's position. I would explain my theological and pastoral problems to the elders and ask them henceforth to present the congregation's position concerning the rebaptism of adults requesting membership. My way of implementing this decision was to request that the elders study the relationship of baptism and membership with the possibility that the congregation's official position could be changed. The discussion seemed to be moving in the direction I hoped, although my pastoral leadership, unbeknownst to me, was soon to be rejected by leaders of the congregation. One of the first decisions when a new pastor came to the congregation was to reaffirm its traditional closed-membership position. The Barrett Avenue Christian Church in Richmond, California, where I became a part-time member of staff while beginning my doctoral studies at Pacific School of Religion, was quietly open membership, and my membership ever since has been in open-membership congregations.

A Church Truly Catholic, Truly Evangelical, and Truly Reformed

Although my doctoral studies did not focus on ecclesial or sacramental topics, I did come across ideas that related to my continuing reflections on Christian baptism, including an analysis by Friedrich Schleiermacher, an influential nineteenth-century theologian. He drew a close connection between the two sides of regeneration—the inward workings of the Holy Spirit in the life of a person and the rite of baptism, which Christ himself had enjoined as the means of receiving a person into the life of the church. Schleiermacher stated that, ideally, the two aspects would be identical in time, but he acknowledged that "it is undeniably in the nature of the case that the inclination of the Church to baptize will sometimes run ahead of the inward workings of the Spirit for regeneration and sometimes lag behind them."[11]

This idea made enough sense to me that I used it in a presentation at Grace Episcopal Cathedral in San Francisco, where I was serving on a panel representing several sacramental traditions. The idea was well-received by the Episcopalians who were participants in the seminar. While I could not detect any tendency among them to discontinue the practice of infant baptism, they expressed a greater openness to adult baptism than they would have manifested prior to hearing that idea. Schleiermacher thus provided me a way to recommend believer baptism while at the same time accepting the efficacy of infant baptism. Although I rarely referred to Schleiermacher's idea in my seminary teaching, it was a critical factor in allowing me to maintain an open stance toward infant baptism in my work with students in churches with that practice.

During the years I was studying in Berkeley, events took place that would henceforth provide the context for my continuing

---

[11] Friedrich Schleiermacher, *The Christian Faith*, edited by H. R. McIntosh and J. S. Stewart (Edinburgh, Scotland: T. & T. Clark, 1928), 623.

reflections on the Disciples' vocation of Christian unity. In December 1960, the National Council of Churches held its general assembly in San Francisco. On Sunday, December 4, immediately prior to the assembly's opening session, Eugene Carson Blake, the activist leader of the United Presbyterian Church, was the guest preacher at Grace Cathedral, where nationally known James A. Pike was the bishop. Blake proposed that their two churches invite the Methodist Church and the United Church of Christ to join them in exploring the possibility of creating a united church that would, from the outset, be truly catholic and truly reformed. His presupposition was that these four churches were essentially agreed on the fundamentals of the Christian faith, sacraments, and ministry and could achieve this goal in a relatively brief time.

It was disheartening that my church, with its historic commitment to Christian unity, was left out of this proposal. Perhaps neither Blake nor Pike with their East- and West-Coast orientations was aware of Disciples, whose strength was in the Midwest and South. They may have felt that Disciples would be difficult partners because of their commitment to believer baptism. The most unsettling possibility was that Blake and Pike discounted the approach to unity they associated with Disciples. In 1962, the four churches invited the Disciples and the Evangelical United Brethren Church, each of which was already engaged in union conversations with one of the four participating churches, to join the consultation.

By this time, I had taken my place on the faculty of Christian Theological Seminary, which put me in regular contact with Ronald E. Osborn, who was one of the Disciples delegates. Both in his public presentations and in our private conversations, he conveyed the sense of excitement and the shape of theological discussion that were emerging in the consultation. The prospects for creating a united church, embracing the center of American life, seemed strong. The early documents coming from the consultation were visionary and practical, calling the churches to an organic unity that would make all of us more complete than we could ever hope to be if we remained separated. They suggested that we would all be able to retain those aspects of our traditions that linked us to the apostles, were treasured in our respective memories, and promised to be useful as the church fulfilled its purposes in the coming generations.

These documents taught that the only thing we would have to give up would be our separation.[12]

The central purpose of the churches participating in the consultation was the resolve to "attempt, under God, a more inclusive expression of the oneness of the Church of Christ than any of the participating churches can suppose itself to be alone."[13] Two principles were to guide their work—that they "be true to every essential link with the apostolic gospel and community," and that they "guard every opportunity of action that will assist us better to bear responsibility for the future."[14] COCU's "Open Letter to the Churches" was candid in confessing the fact that the churches' separation from one another, despite God's intention that they be one, weakened their witness to the gospel. The delegates acknowledged that even the anticipated union would still be limited in its capacity to express the oneness of the Church of Christ. The union they were seeking to develop would be marked by fidelity to the scriptures, a credible confession of the Christian faith, public worship and sacramental life that expressed clearly the "high priesthood of Christ," and a ministry whose gifts would be released for "wider and more effective service."[15] All of these characteristics would enable the united church to multiply the effectiveness of mission in the world.

Even more important than the "Open Letter" was the document entitled, "Principles of Church Union," which the consultation adopted in 1966. In four short chapters, each of them not much longer than a sermon, "Principles" described the faith, worship, sacraments, and ministry of the church that the delegates believed God was calling upon them to create. More than any other contemporary document, this slender volume summed up the central core of the Christian faith in language that mainstream Christians could affirm.

Unity discussions took on a new character during a three-year period, beginning in 1966, when three African American

---

[12] Although I thought the idea had been expressed in an earlier COCU document, the earliest I can now find is in *A Plan of Union for the Church of Christ Uniting* (Princeton, NJ: Consultation on Church Union, 1970), 12. The statement reads: "Visible unity should take away from us nothing essential; we will lose only our separateness."

[13] *Consultation on Church Union 1967: Principles of Church Union, Guidelines for Structure, and a Study Guide* (Cincinnati, OH: Forward Movement Publications, 1967), 21.

[14] Ibid., 15.

[15] Ibid., 22.

Methodist churches became full participants in the consultation. Each of these churches had emerged in the nineteenth century when Black members of Methodist congregations had withdrawn from predominately White Methodist churches so that Black members could be fully involved in every aspect of church life. Their coming into the consultation called attention to the fact that many of the divisions of the church were caused by societal and cultural factors rather than by theological or sacramental differences. From this time onward, the consultation devoted as much attention to issues of race, culture, and condition in life as it did to the traditional factors of faith, sacraments, and ministry.

My direct participation in the consultation began in 1968, when I was appointed to join prominent pastor Colbert S. Cartwright as the second Disciple in COCU's commission on worship. This responsibility qualified me to attend COCU's plenary assemblies, which took place each spring, and for two decades I maintained an active presence in these meetings. The Disciples delegation included the central leaders of our church—the executives of the most important agencies, pastors of tall-steeple churches, and academicians. They impressed me by their theological grasp of the issues being debated and their competency as representatives of the Christian Church (Disciples of Christ). I was especially impressed by A. Dale Fiers, general minister and president of the Christian Church; George Beazley, president of the Council on Christian Unity; and my faculty colleague, Ronald E. Osborn. Three pastors also impressed me because of their theological acumen and their strong sense of the character of the Disciples tradition: Walter Bingham, an African American pastor from Louisville; W. J. Jarman, from Champaign, Illinois; and Colbert S. Cartwright, from Youngstown, Ohio (and later Fort Worth, Texas).

It quickly became evident that the delegations from other churches also included top leadership—the people who had access to the levers of power among the major Protestant denominations of that era. If any church leaders could bring about union, these delegates to the Consultation on Church Union were the ones who could do it. I was especially interested in how the Disciples delegation acted when voting. They made little effort to consult with one another; yet their individual votes seemed amazingly alike. It was as if they instinctively knew how Disciples should respond to the idea.

As he prepared for the Consultation's 1967-68 convocation, Seattle pastor David G. Colwell, was interviewed by Ray Rupert, Religion Editor of the *Seattle Times*. He declared his conviction that the union which the churches were seeking to create would take place by the time he retired, within fourteen years. [16] Although Colwell retired on schedule, the union did not take place. The "Principles" sketched a design, but in order for the churches to move toward union, a more detailed program had to be developed. In 1970, the Consultation approved *A Plan of Union for the Church of Christ Uniting*. The *Plan of Union* expanded the exposition of the church's faith, worship, sacraments, and ministry. It was the first step in a process that led to longer, more complicated theological statements that served to impede union rather than facilitate it.

The *Plan of Union* also presented detailed proposals concerning the organization of the Church of Christ Uniting. Although it was necessary that this be done, the ideas put forward became deterrents to the process. Delegates to COCU during its early years were aware of the disparities between congregations in central cities and those in suburbs. In most places, inner-city congregations were located in areas of blight and were themselves reduced in membership and resources from their times of great strength. In contrast, suburban congregations were in areas that were experiencing growth and improving socio-economic conditions. The contrast between central city and suburban communities also had a strong racial component that was exhibited in the makeup of churches across these zones. Delegates to COCU were committed to developing a church that in its local manifestations could overcome economic, cultural, and racial disparities.

The *Plan of Union* proposed that the "front-line expression of church life where people live and work" be a parish that connected several congregations together. The full range of local church life would take place within the parish, thus freeing congregations from the burden of having to "attempt a full program of worship,

---

[16] Colwell was pastor of Plymouth Congregational Church in downtown Seattle. His COCU presidency included 1967–1968, the year that I was on research leave at University Christian Church in Seattle. The interview was published in the *Seattle Times*, March 25, 1968.

education at every level, fellowship, and action."[17] This idea was inspired, in part, by the writings of sociologist Gibson Winter, who had proposed that congregations be linked in groups that cut across a city's economic and racial zones.[18] Each group would be governed by a parish board that would distribute financial resources and assign staff leadership wherever it was needed to the congregations in that parish.

Although this proposal to redefine the local unit of the church was commendable, it never had a chance of succeeding. One reason was its failure to recognize the significance to most people of their relationships within their congregations. It became clear that the local unit of the church was created and maintained by the experience of worshiping together. The sense of Christian identity formed in congregations could not be transferred to the larger, less experiential parishes. A second reason for failure was the unwillingness of congregations to distribute resources according to the principles of the new model. Even the churches with centralized control, such as the Methodist bodies, could not develop an effective trans-congregational sharing of resources. How, then, could the weaker structures of the united church expect to do it? A third reason was that the racial conflicts within American society were too deeply engrained even in the COCU churches for them to be able to create parishes that necessarily would be interracial.

The *Plan of Union* also offered a process whereby participating churches would consolidate their organizational structures and create a new ecclesiastical organization. The consultation had already rejected one idea—that a new national judicatory be established that would take on the functions of the highest governing structure of each of the participating churches while the lesser organizations, agencies, and judicatories of the denominations continued.[19] In the *Plan of Union*, the delegates to the consultation, most of them high-level executives and officers of their churches, proposed a more

---

[17] *A Plan of Union of Union for the Church of Christ Uniting* (Princeton, NJ: Consultation on Church Union, 1970), 56–57.

[18] Gibson Winter. *The Suburban Captivity of the Churches: An Analysis of Protestant Responsibility in the Expanding Metropolis* (Garden City, NY: Doubleday, 1961).

[19] The term *judicatory* was borrowed from Presbyterians and refers to any and all of the councils, conferences, districts, and synods by which the churches govern themselves.

complex process, including the creation of a transitional national assembly and the subsequent formation of transitional regions that would take over the responsibilities previously carried by the many parallel judicatories of all of the uniting churches.

The *Plan of Union* was sent to the churches for study and comment. By the end of the two-year study period, it was clear that, although COCU continued, its *Plan of Union* was dead. The Consultation decided to continue expanding the theological and sacramental aspects on which the churches already were significantly agreed. It also established two processes that were designed to draw the churches closer together. Generating communities were to be groups of congregations that would covenant with one another to "work together in mission and to be a community committed to service, justice, inclusiveness, and unity."[20] Interim eucharistic fellowships would bring "COCU-related congregations together regularly to study and pray for 'the unity Christ wills among us' and to celebrate the Lord's supper as a sign of 'the unity Christ has given us.'"[21]

Together these two ventures would provide connections on a voluntary basis that would parallel the connections that parishes in the *Plan of Union* would have mandated. My impression was that Paul A. Crow Jr., the Disciples church historian who was the chief executive of COCU, was the initiator of the idea of the interim eucharistic fellowship. Certainly, he was the person who most vigorously promoted the idea among the COCU delegates.

It would have been appropriate for me as professor of worship and director of the chapel at the seminary to initiate an interim eucharistic fellowship. Congregations representing most of the COCU churches were located in Indianapolis. The seminary and I had good relations with church leaders, and we were ideally placed to be a focal point for COCU in Indianapolis. My own interest in the Eucharist should have pushed me into action. Yet, I did not; nor did anyone else in our city work with any seriousness on these matters. An opportunity missed!

At this point, COCU's momentum slowed and as it did the denominational delegations began to change. In most of them the

---

[20] Paul A. Crow Jr., "Ecumenical Lessons from COCU's History, 1960–1995," *Mid-Stream* 34, no. 3 (July/August 1995), 33.
[21] Ibid.

top decision makers began drifting away and other members of staffs were appointed in their places. Although I was disheartened by the change of mood and the loss of momentum, I was generally satisfied with the contents of the theological statements that emerged and were sent to the churches as *A Plan of Union*.[22] As might be expected, I was most interested in the chapter titled, "This People at Worship," in which the consultation offered a strong affirmation of the importance of worship and claimed the forms of worship, liturgical books, and traditions of all of the participating churches. This chapter also said that the united church would "encourage in every parish the experimental use and interpretations of the liturgies of all the united churches and traditions in order to increase mutual understanding and enrichment."[23]

The discussion of baptism, however, demonstrated the difficulty of creating one church out of denominations with divergent convictions and practices. The general statement about the sacraments was consistent with the classic Disciples' conviction that God is at work in baptism: "A sacrament ... is an effective sign, symbol, or seal; it not only signifies, but also, by God's gift, conveys that which it signifies."[24] Disciples could also agree that "there is but one baptism," but would be made uneasy by the acceptance in the *Plan of Union* of various modes of baptism, and they would find the rite itself more detailed than they were accustomed to. The assertion that "both infant baptism and the baptism of consenting believers shall be maintained as alternative practices within the united church" was balanced by the statement that "neither shall be imposed contrary to conscience."[25] Furthermore, the *Plan of Union* stated that the united church would provide "for those baptized a solemn act of confirming baptismal vows."[26] My marginal notes indicate how I felt about the paragraph dealing with confirmation, "so ambiguous as to be of no value."

George Beazley, the Disciples' ecumenical officer, must have responded more positively to that paragraph in the *Plan of Union* because he stated that Disciples could accept infant baptism only

---

[22] *A Plan of Union of Union for the Church of Christ Uniting* (Princeton, NJ: Consultation on Church Union, 1970).
[23] Ibid., 31.
[24] Ibid., 33.
[25] Ibid., 34.
[26] Ibid., 35.

because the united church would also practice confirmation before people could be admitted to the Lord's supper. Although I agreed that this insistence would ease the transition for Disciples, I also was aware that discussions in the Commission on worship were undercutting this provision. Scholars in the field of sacramental and liturgical theology were already moving toward reuniting baptism and confirmation, which had once been two parts of a single rite. Furthermore, they were urging churches that practiced infant baptism to admit these children to the table at as early an age as was pastorally possible. The commission on worship was preparing "An Order for the Celebration of Holy Baptism," in which these new ideas were being expressed in the liturgical materials and in the commentary. Thus, the Consultation's baptismal liturgy was proposing a course of action that differed from the one described in the *Plan of Union*.

My interest in and knowledge of liturgical developments concerning baptism and confirmation were heightened by my role in COCU's commission on worship, which culminated in the 1973 publication of *Holy Baptism*.[27] H. Boone Porter, an Episcopal priest and scholar who taught liturgics at General Theological Seminary in New York, wrote the introduction and prepared the bibliography, which together filled most of the book. After referring to the "many historical, biblical, theological, and pastoral studies [that] have recently been devoted to this topic," Porter stated that "the publication of a new rite" could not solve the relationship between baptism and confirmation.[28] He pointed out that this new liturgy was a complete rite, "containing baptism in water, the invocation of the Holy Spirit with laying on of hands, and Holy Communion."[29] The commission's intention was that the complete rite be conducted whenever possible, and the commentary made suggestions that could guide churches as they made decisions based on the disciplines of their churches and other pastoral considerations.

I drafted the liturgy and found this responsibility to be especially interesting and satisfying because it offered me the opportunity of preparing a service of Christian baptism, in an ecumenical context,

---

[27] Consultation on Church Union, *An Order for the Celebration of Holy Baptism with Commentary* (Cincinnati, OH: Forward Movement Publications, 1973).
[28] Ibid., 23.
[29] Ibid.

that presupposed believer baptism to be the norm. The rite was much fuller and more complete than the traditional Disciples' pattern, which, as my Disciples colleague Colbert S. Cartwright had observed, was liturgically and pastorally thin when compared with rites in other churches. One of my disappointments was that the commission did not accept my first effort to write the pastoral statement with which the rite began. I had been reading one of the classic books on the history of religion in which the author noted that in ancient times initiatory rites were not aesthetic ceremonies. Rather, they transmitted power from the religious community to the initiate.[30] At the time, I was the Sunday ad interim preacher at a strong Disciples congregation in the Indianapolis suburb of Zionsville. With that congregation in mind, I asked myself what new power the people were seeking as they came to that church. My conclusion was that they wanted to find a foundation for personal security and peace. Without doing any exegetical work, I decided to adapt Jesus's statement from the gospel of John (14:27). Although I no longer have the original text that I sent to the commission, I wrote a declaration by the minister of the service that Jesus offered peace to those who in faith came to him in baptism. Charles W. F. Smith, another Episcopal delegate to the commission and professor of New Testament at Episcopal Divinity School in Cambridge, Massachusetts, rejected that use of John, and I had to develop another text to begin the liturgy.

Nearly a decade after the publication of *Holy Baptism*, while on a family visit in Florida, my wife, Billie Watkins, and I were attending the Presbyterian church where our son Michael and his family were active participants. Our son-in-law, Richard Lowery, who had been reared in the acapella Churches of Christ, was one of our family group. During the morning service, a young couple brought their infant daughter to be baptized. As the pastor began the liturgy, I recognized the text. He was using the COCU baptismal liturgy, which meant that the first service of infant baptism Rick had ever witnessed was one that had been written by his Disciples father-in-law.

Another part of the *Plan of Union* that I believed would be difficult for Disciples was the chapter titled, "To Be Ministers of Christ." One of its provisions was for the reconciling and uniting of

---

[30] G. van der Leeuw, *Religion in Essence and Manifestation* (New York: Harper Torchbook, 1963).

the ordained ministries of the participating churches—the ministry of the Episcopal Church ordained in "apostolic succession" and the ministries of all of the rest of us. I was content with the provision that there would be "a corporate act through which all will offer the existing ministries to Almighty God, asking him to receive them through Jesus Christ, to complete and perfect what is amiss or incomplete in them, and to give them whatever of his authority and grace is needed to serve in the united ministry."[31] I feared, however, that many Disciples would be offended by the need for any rite of reconciliation.

Difficulties of a different kind could be anticipated as the uniting churches dealt with Disciples elders who regularly presided at the Eucharist even though in most congregations they had not been ordained. The participating churches, as well as most other churches around the world, insisted that ordination was required of all who would preside at the Lord's table. The discussion was complicated by the fact that some of the other churches also used the title of elder, but the title meant different things. Among Methodists, elder was the title given to ordained ministers with full authority to administer word and sacraments. Presbyterians had teaching elders and ruling elders who were ordained with the same rite but given different authority. The ruling elders corresponded to Disciples elders, but they could not preside at the Eucharist. At first, the other churches seemed willing, in principle, to accept Disciples elders but only if they were ordained.

Some Disciples delegates, with George Beazley their leader, affirmed that this procedure was consistent with early Disciples understandings of the eldership and should be supported. Other Disciples delegates, however, were unfavorable toward the idea that our elders be ordained and thus be given a rank within the clergy of the united church. On one occasion, I spoke to the COCU plenary on this issue, proposing that the rapidly changing missionary context that our churches were entering called for an office of non-salaried sacramental leaders of the churches. My comments were affirmed by an Episcopal bishop, who used his church's experience among Inuit people as support. Presbyterian and Methodist spokespersons, however, were strongly opposed.

---

[31] *A Plan of Union*, 44.

I do not remember that this issue was ever settled in a public formal manner. Rather, it gradually faded from view, and later documents clearly affirmed that presiding at the Eucharist was one of the functions of ordained presbyters, which is the term that had been chosen as the COCU alternative to priest, elder, pastor, and minister. Although the documents did not insist that presbyters had to be salaried officers of churches, they presumed that prevailing patterns would be carried into the united church. Disciples elders, one could easily conclude, would probably disappear from the Church of Christ Uniting.

The COCU discussions of the ministry prompted Ronald E. Osborn, who was the theological leader of the Disciples delegation, to do extensive research on the office of ministry as it is described in the New Testament. In an extended note in the book that resulted, he stated that he did not "view with abhorrence" an occasion when the church appoints carefully chosen, mature lay persons to preside at the table and offer the prayers of thanksgiving. He acknowledged, however, that this practice obscured "the proper function of the public ministry," threatened a church's understanding "of the corporate responsibility for good order," and went counter to "the almost unanimous weight of Christian tradition." Therefore, he confessed that he was ready to forego the traditional Disciples eldership for the sake of good order in a united church.[32] I do not recall what Disciples delegates had to say about the church leaders whom Disciples call licensed lay ministers. Already, regional ministers and congregations were developing ways for these committed lay members of the churches to take on ministerial roles, in some cases becoming the called pastors of congregations.

My conclusion, as I have reflected upon this development, is that the licensed lay ministers have become a close counterpart to the elders in the early years of the Christian Church movement. They come into prominence in a congregation, gradually assuming greater leadership, especially in worship leadership and pastoral care, and then take a study program that acquaints them with the Bible and introductory aspects of theology and church leadership. Some licensed lay ministers continue with that same congregation and become, in effect, volunteer assistant ministers. Others are

---

[32] Ronald E. Osborn. *In Christ's Place: Christian Ministry in Today's World* (St. Louis: Bethany Press, 1967), 258–259.

approved for pastoral leadership in another congregation and become the designated, salaried pastor, even though they have not been ordained. Either form of service, however, could be understood as a faithful representation of the original Disciples' view of the eldership.

Throughout most of the COCU process, apostolic succession was a problem, despite the fact that one of the first principles of the consultation, explicitly stated by Presbyterian Eugene Carson Blake in the sermon that started the process, was that the ministry of the united church would be in apostolic succession. He meant that the united church would have bishops ordained by other bishops in that succession. Most of the participating churches, including Disciples, already had officers whose functions were closely parallel to the functions of bishops in the Episcopal Church and other catholic churches. Presbyterian churches, however, were led by what some called the "corporate episcopate," the teaching elders and ruling elders of the congregations meeting in presbytery. Everyone, including Presbyterians, knew that Presbyterians would have to find a way for one person, perhaps chosen by presbytery, to be ordained in apostolic succession and function as the officer of ordination. Although Blake clearly understood this provision, as did other Presbyterian delegates during COCU's early years, there has been little evidence that Presbyterians would be willing to make this change.

Disciples would also be challenged by this need to reshape traditional procedures in order to conform to the *Plan of Union*. Although Disciples regional ministers functioned in ways that paralleled the work of Episcopal bishops, they were not in apostolic succession; nor were they the mandated officers for ordination. It was common practice among Disciples for someone from the regional commission on the ministry and someone from the regional staff to participate in ordination services. Sometimes the regional minister was that person, but few Disciples believed that the regional minister had to be present and lay hands on all ordinands in order for Disciples to bring their practice into conformity with the consensus among most churches of Christendom.

In the late 1980s, I was one of nine people on a working group representing the Disciples' Council on Christian Unity, Homeland Ministries, the regions, and pastors. Our purpose was to develop guidelines for ordination that could be recommended to Disciples everywhere. Also serving on the working group were Paul A. Crow Jr., the longtime president of the Council on Christian Unity, and Robert K. Welsh, who had for many years been Crow's associate on the council. The group represented a rather wide range of ideas about ordination. Everyone agreed that there was a need to bring order to the process across the nation. We were not agreed about the importance of bringing Disciples' practice into conformity with COCU's ecumenical vision.

The one regional minister on the working group, C. Edward Weisheimer of Indiana, insisted that we had to allow for the diversity of conviction and tradition that already existed in Disciples regions. Our document referred frequently to responsibilities of regional ministers, but we had to allow for the fact that regional ministers often would not be the officer of ordination: "The regional minister, by the nature of the office, represents the region which authorizes ordination. Therefore, the regional minister, or designated alternate, ordinarily presides over the act of ordination."[33]

On December 9, 1988, the official delegates to the seventeenth plenary assembly of the Consultation on Church Union approved a document titled, "Churches in Covenant Communion," and commended it to their respective churches. Four years earlier, delegates had taken similar action with a document titled, *The COCU Consensus*. These two documents were being proposed as the basis for the nine participating communions to form a new ecclesial body— The Church of Christ Uniting. I was an interested observer at this meeting in New Orleans because of my work as primary drafter of the liturgies that were included in "Churches in Covenant Communion." COCU's commission on worship had been asked to develop the liturgical texts that would be used to inaugurate the new united church. After considerable work, we had presented our first drafts to the 1984 plenary; following study and response by the churches, the commission on worship revised the texts for the 1988 gathering. We offered three liturgies—national, regional, and local—with some parts in common and others distinctive to a particular liturgy. All of the liturgies included prayers of confession and intercession,

---

[33] *Ordination Service and Guidelines for Ordination for the Christian Church (Disciples of Christ)* (Indianapolis: Council on Christian Unity and Homeland Ministries, 1990), 7.

readings from the Bible, a sermon, and the celebration of the Eucharist. We drew on other liturgies that COCU had developed and adapted language from the agreements that churches had made with one another. Members of the worship commission were assigned drafting responsibilities, and then we sought to bring this material into a theologically adequate, smoothly flowing liturgical form. Most reviewers agreed that the commission did quite well with the content of the liturgies; many also said, however, that the language needed more life and color. Even though I did much of the shaping of these texts, I agree that they lack color and energy.

One action—declaring the covenant—was especially important because it would bring the participating churches into a new public relationship with one another. Following the Service of the Word, all of the liturgies had a section titled "Declaring the Covenant." Representatives of the participating churches would make a series of seven declarations concerning how they would act toward one another from this time forward. The conclusion to these statements was this declaration: "By our covenant, our churches now recognize each other as true Churches of Jesus Christ, as authentic expressions of the one, holy, catholic, and apostolic Church." This statement was followed immediately by a series of six affirmations that are made by the congregants. This new relationship was expressed by the exchange of the peace of Christ and by prayers of intercession for the world.

In order for this declaration to take force, the ministries of the participating churches had to be reconciled with one another. At one level, the change was simple enough. Although the ministers had previously worked in their respective denominations, separated from one another, they were kept apart primarily by custom and administrative procedures. In the new church, the institutional separations would be largely set aside and the reconciled ministries would henceforth minister together as one body. At another level, however, reconciliation was much more difficult, for it had to lead the churches over the seismic fault of apostolic succession. Some ministers had been ordained in apostolic succession as it was maintained within the Episcopal Church. For them, the question was whether ministers ordained some other way were authentic ministers. Historically, the common answer to this question had been that those ordinations were in some serious way insufficient.

Now the people in apostolic succession would publicly affirm the full, authentic ministry of people whose ordinations previously had been considered irregular, and perhaps even defective. The ministers whose churches did not stand in apostolic succession, confident that their ministries were valid and effective, faced a different challenge: Could they, in good conscience, participate in a liturgy of reconciliation that in any way implied that their ordinations had been irregular or deficient?

The form we proposed for the liturgies of reconciliation had four elements. Each participating church would put forward all of its ministers who had been chosen and ordained according to the practices of that church. All participating ministers then would renew their vows and pray that God would complete in them the gifts they needed for ministry and enable them to minister together in unity. In silence, the ministers would have hands laid upon them—as had been done at their ordinations—but the liturgies gave this action a different meaning: Instead of conferring the Holy Spirit and the office of ministry, the sign in these liturgies of reconciliation conveys forgiveness, welcome, and the sharing of ministries with one another. Following the silent laying on of hands, now understood to be a sign of reconciliation, participants would offer prayers in unison. They would ask God to complete in them the gifts for ministry that had been received and exercised in their separation so that they could minister together as ministers in God's church.

Although I no longer can separate my contributions from those of others on the drafting team, I do remember our feeling that we on the commission on worship were leading the way for the official delegates in the Consultation, showing how liturgical action would be the vehicle for our churches to move into closer union.

As I prepared to attend the 1988 plenary assembly, I wrote a paper summing up some of my reflections about the process that had occupied so much of my time and for which I had worked diligently. I noted three aspects of the twenty-year process that were especially interesting to me. The first was the importance of apostolicity—a direct and continuing connection with the faith, witness, and life of the first leaders of the church. When we could declare that each of the churches possessed this quality, then we could proceed in good faith. The second factor was the great difficulty in giving organizational embodiment to the consultation's social vision—whether that be a new ecclesial form for the church or a way of life that transcends the barriers of gender, class, and race. Despite our vision and persistent efforts, vested interests and the deeply engrained social factors of American life continued to resist every effort to overcome them. My third reflection was that, despite the slow progress toward achieving organic union, people in a wide range of churches were experiencing an ever-stronger sense of unity with one another. I remembered how separated Catholics and Protestants were prior to the Second Vatican Council and that, early in my ministry, mainstream Protestants usually enjoyed good relations with one another, but often found themselves as separated from Episcopalians and Lutherans as from Catholics. They now were living together with a mutuality that had previously not been present.

I concluded my 1988 reflections by stating my gratitude for the advances toward Christian unity that had taken place during my years of ministry and disappointment that we had reached this stage of COCU's life with so little to show for all the work and all the money sacrificed to this dream. American denominations, I asserted, were intractable. During these COCU decades, Presbyterians, Disciples, and the United Church of Christ had relocated headquarters buildings, two of these churches moving to different cities from where they had been before. Yet each had insisted on reestablishing itself in a city of its own. Even in this period when the mainline denominations had dwindled away, none of them was willing to relinquish its identity, institutional memory, or place in the American landscape. Covenant communion might ease relations at the level of sacraments, worship, and ministry—and perhaps mission—but many of the dreams of this venture in unity remained unrealized. Perhaps they were not even hoped for by a generation that did not experience the excitement with which this vision broke onto the American landscape.

Five years after I had written this personal reflection and distributed it privately among a few friends, Paul A. Crow Jr. remembered it and asked to include the essay in an issue of *Mid-Stream* that would bear the title "The Promise of the Consultation on Church Union."[34]

---

[34] Keith Watkins, "Twenty Years with the Consultation on Church Union" in *Mid-Stream* 34, no. 3 (July/October 1995): 93–103. The paragraphs above are adapted from this publication.

Churches Uniting in Christ

Nearly seven years later, in January 2002, when we met in Memphis for the inauguration of the Churches Uniting in Christ, Gerald F. Moede, who for many years had been COCU's general secretary and a close colleague in COCU activities, asked me if I still felt the disappointment that had been expressed in the *Mid-Stream* essay. He hoped, I supposed, that the actions we had come to celebrate on that winter weekend had given me cause for a more positive evaluation of this long and twisting movement toward realizing more fully the unity of these churches at the heart of American life and culture.

He was right to expect that I might feel more positive in 2002 than I had in 1988 or 1995, because we had come to Memphis, along with some 300 other members of the COCU churches, to conclude the Consultation on Church Union and inaugurate something new—Churches Uniting in Christ (CUIC). In a plenary assembly in 1999, and by subsequent official actions in their respective assemblies, the COCU churches had decided to become CUIC, thus continuing their work in a new way. Instead of remaining a consultation, they would become a communion of churches that were bound to one another in faith, worship, ministry, and mission. In a series of public assemblies, beginning in Memphis, representatives of these churches would mutually recognize one another's churches as authentic expressions of the one church of Jesus Christ—this on the basis of agreements that had been hammered out through long periods of discussion during the decades of COCU's life. They would commit their churches to live together in ways that expressed their unity in Christ ever more clearly and effectively.

Although this new relationship was expected to impact the organizational systems of these churches, institutional union—the merger of nine churches into one—was no longer a goal of the relationship. The transformation from a consultation to a communion of churches would take place despite the fact that these churches could not yet declare themselves in full communion, for the issues related to ministry, which Eugene Carson Blake had intended to resolve at the beginning of the process, had still not been settled, with Presbyterians and Episcopalians representing the two sides to the debate.

In preparation for the convocation in Memphis, COCU's executive committee asked me to draft the liturgy the churches would use to make their declarations to one another. Although it would be based on the 1988 liturgies, which I and the COCU commission on worship had drafted, this new draft would express the changes that had taken place since 1988. It was to include a significantly stronger declaration of the commitment to combat racism in church and society. After Michael Kinnamon, who had become the general secretary of the Consultation, had reviewed a draft, I sent a revision to a meeting of COCU's executive committee and the program committee preparing for Memphis. In a strong, extended discussion of the text, the program committee affirmed the work, but with several recommendations for strengthening the liturgy. Although three or four members of the group promised to review my revisions, only one did so. Two friends with strong liturgical sensitivities also commented on my drafts as I moved to completion. Early in 2001, I sent my completed draft to Kinnamon and the program committee, and with only two or three minor emendations, my draft provided the words and actions for the major liturgy on Sunday, January 20, 2002.

At first, I thought that I would not attend the Memphis convocation, but as the date came closer, I decided to attend and enjoy, as best I could, my status as elder statesman. It would differ greatly from other plenary assemblies I had attended. There would be no debate, as the decisions had all been made. In a ceremonial business meeting over dinner, the churches would take two actions: They would create CUIC and close down COCU. Following dinner, everyone would adjourn to the Episcopal Church's St. Mary's Cathedral to celebrate the Eucharist one last time as the Consultation on Church Union, using the 1985 liturgy that the commission on worship had drafted.

Sunday afternoon we would assemble at Mt. Olive Cathedral of the Christian Methodist Episcopal Church for the inaugural liturgy, culminating in the Eucharist, using the new text that I had drafted. On Monday morning, we would join city officials and other citizens of Memphis for a march to the Lorraine Motel, where Martin Luther King Jr. had been slain. There, leaders of the CUIC churches would sign a document pledging their churches to combat and eradicate racism in America.

Three words described my attitude as the Memphis convocation approached. I felt *appreciation* for my many years working for Christian unity through the Consultation and for the challenging privilege of revising and extending that commission's work in the inaugural liturgy. Even stronger was my sense of *gratitude* that after forty years of work this effort to develop a more visible form of Christian unity in the United States had reached its climax stage and was settling into a new way of continuing into the future. My strongest feeling, however, as I told Gerald Moede, was *melancholy* that this new relationship was so limited in its impact on the inner life of the participating churches and on American society.

After arriving at the assembly in Memphis, and during the first day of its activities, I found my melancholy developing a more hopeful cast. The most important reason was the announcement that a new partner in mission and dialogue was coming into CUIC. Throughout COCU's life, two streams of the sixteenth-century Reformation have been involved—the Episcopal-Methodist and the Reformed. Only a few weeks before the Memphis convocation, the Evangelical Lutheran Church of America had decided to enter into this relationship, which meant that a third Reformation stream was becoming part of the process in a newly defined relationship. Although the fourth major branch of the Reformation, the Anabaptist, was not yet in sight, the coming in of the major American manifestation of the Lutheran heritage significantly broadened the movement toward fuller union.

A second reason for hope was the announcement that a process for "cutting the Gordian knot" of the historic episcopate had been launched. Although the initial proposal leading to the Consultation included the declaration, by Presbyterian Eugene Carson Blake, that the new church would have bishops in apostolic succession, the Presbyterian and Episcopal churches had not been able to resolve their respective reservations concerning a ministry that would lead to full communion of the churches. After their delegations had come to Memphis, the representatives of these two churches committed themselves to a bilateral dialogue for the express purpose of resolving this issue on behalf of all of the churches in CUIC.

I was also encouraged by the fact that the churches in CUIC were obviously making progress in overcoming two of the "isms" that separate the churches and divide American society. Sexism, expressed in the exclusion of women from leadership in the churches, was fading, although men continued to dominate the major places of leadership, as was demonstrated by the solid phalanx of men in the Monday morning ceremony at the Lorraine Motel. Even so, an increasing body of women had moved into positions of leadership throughout the participating churches. And racism, which assigns worth and determines opportunity primarily on the basis of race, has also eased within the churches, although continuing to be a far stronger factor than the prominence of people of color in the signing ceremony at the Lorraine Motel implied.

Another cause for my new hope was the realization that younger people in the churches could still be excited by the possibilities of more visible unity. Although the number of seminarians at the Memphis assembly was quite small—perhaps twenty persons, representing only four seminaries out of more than fifty related to the COCU churches—they exuded an excitement similar to my own when this process had begun during my years as a graduate student in Berkeley.

The fact that these churches were continuing their movement toward more visible unity, it seemed to me as I thought about this weekend, was confirming certain aspects of their identity that made them part of the American mainstream. Historically, all of them held theological positions that were poised between authoritarian traditions and secularism. For more than a century, this middle ground had been the essential factor in American liberal theology and an important characteristic of most of the churches in CUIC. In their theological and ethical debates, the CUIC churches were continuing to manifest this flexible intellectual position that would enable them to maintain an important witness to American society.

The Churches Uniting in Christ were continuing patterns of worship rooted in the classic tradition of word and sacrament. Even though many congregations of the participating churches—including Lindenwood Christian Church, which I attended that Sunday morning—have been developing liturgies based on revivalist models, thus repeating the experiments of the 1960s in new forms, their most characteristic liturgies still were focused on pulpit, table, and font. One reason for this liturgical continuity was the fact that CUIC itself and most of the participating churches have been maintaining and strengthening their links with the Roman Catholic Church while that church was increasingly mainline in its relations to American society.

Another way that CUIC was confirming the character of these churches was its emphasis on mission directed toward the major issues and institutions of American public life. The churches participating in this movement toward more visible union have always understood their mission as both devotional–personal and prophetic–public. Despite the constant temptation for them to become sanctuaries of the upper classes, the churches in CUIC have made the recovery of their prophetic–public ministry one of the signs of their faithfulness to Christ and their unity with one another.

Despite the importance of the covenants established in Memphis, several matters would require continued thought and, perhaps even more than discursive reason, they would require persistent prayer. Even in the brief periods of discussion in Memphis, it was clear that ancient wounds were continuing to generate pathogens in the bloodstream. In a discussion concerning the Presbyterian–Anglican debate over corporate and personal forms of episcopal oversight, for example, a church historian from the United Church of Christ observed that ancient and bloody battles over these matters in England and Scotland, although rarely in the conscious mind, continue to generate passion and conflict. Realizing that many of the people at the Memphis convocation had not yet been born when COCU began, I understood with new poignancy that short-term memory in the church was, in fact, very short. Many from the new generation of ecumenists had no knowledge of the provisions in Eugene Carson Blake's initial proposal, and they held a skewed understanding of the central themes of the Consultation on Church Union. Most of the participants in Memphis were not present when COCU tried to solve the problems of polity with ideas such as the extended parish plan, and this failure of short-term memory could easily distort the ongoing discussion concerning organization.

As I listened to people talk, I realized again how difficult it was to distinguish between rite, reason, and routine. While liturgical actions, theological definitions, and systems of governance and mission are always intertwined, each is a discrete aspect of ecclesial life. The churches can hold the Eucharist in high regard even though their theological understandings of this sacrament differ. They can agree on the theological importance of the ministry of the laity even though they express that ministry in significantly different forms of polity. They can affirm the importance of the historic episcopate although they differ in their theological explanations of that practice. Often, however, the factors in the discussion are confused so that, for example, the importance of a theological principle is being defended by insisting on a specific pattern of action.

Another factor for further work and prayer was also evident in Memphis: The churches in CUIC, with their base in the sixteenth-century Reformation, are increasingly separated from the rapidly growing churches with a base in the revivalist or charismatic movements. As important as it may become, CUIC is a movement within one sector of the American religious scene. Many of the largest, most rapidly growing churches represent a radically different approach to shaping the Christian life, church, and mission. Furthermore, during COCU's forty years, the status of the mainstream churches in American life has greatly diminished. Some people have suggested that the move toward more visible unity is inspired by the loss of prestige, as though our coming together would make it possible for these churches to recover prominence that has been lost. Such reasoning, however, has never been a sufficient motivation for establishing a more visible manifestation of unity; and even the greater unity of these churches would be unlikely to bring the return of their former status. Meantime, the need for an effective, intelligent, justice-oriented voice in American society continues to increase.

Despite my commitment to the prophetic–public character of the mainline churches, I left Memphis with an uneasiness concerning the strong focus on overcoming racism that now characterizes this movement of the churches. The pilgrimage to the site where Martin Luther King Jr. was murdered, and the statements made by representatives of the churches constituted one of the emotional high points of the weekend. Racism in American—and especially the institutionalized privilege and power of light-skinned people—still is strong and must be combated. Yet, the struggle against racism can obscure the continuing challenge of other problems—including poverty, war, population growth, and environmental crisis—that are among the other issues that diminish American life, and the churches participating in CUIC must not become single-issue churches. Even King, whose life and work we remembered in the ceremonies at the Lorraine Motel, was moving, at the time of his death, from his primary focus on racism to others, including poverty and the war in Vietnam.

I realized that the crucial developments for Churches Uniting in Christ would take place after people left Memphis and returned to their homes. Delegates would have to lead their churches to bring the life of congregations and denominations into growing consonance with the principles that the churches have affirmed. Since then, however, none of the churches has fulfilled the entire range of principles concerning faith, worship, ministry, and mission they have affirmed in their consultations and declarations. All of them need to keep working on increasing that consonance.

The Memphis actions expressed one way to achieve this goal: to increase the frequency and intensity of relationships in worship and mission among the churches, especially in local communities. The churches were to live their way into greater unity, and to do this they would have to worship and work together, which happens only as the result of constant effort. The communion of these churches, which would lead to greater consonance with the gospel, had to include their working together to overcoming the division-causing factors such as sexism and racism. The history of humankind indicates that every generation has to face these issues. Despite the progress made by the participating churches and American society in past years, these problems continue to plague the churches and the nation. The struggle to establish greater justice is never-ending.

My Disciples Postscript

As the COCU process lumbered along in its later years, I came to three conclusions. The first was that after the first half-dozen years the churches had shifted gears from high-speed overdrive to low-speed mountain drive. The more we labored over consensus documents, the heavier the prose seemed to be and, as a corollary, our chances of persuading the churches and their constituents to create a united church seemed ever weaker. The second conclusion was that, despite the failure to achieve organic union, the COCU process had stimulated these churches to move toward one another in their patterns of thought, worship, ministry, and witness, a movement that probably would not have taken place if we had not been locked together by COCU in the intention to unite institutionally.

The third conclusion, pertinent to me as a Disciple, was that even in their later forms the COCU consensus documents presented a summary statement of the ecclesial and sacramental convictions of the historic Protestant churches stated in the theological language of the late twentieth century. All Disciples who were well read in the writings of Alexander Campbell should therefore have been especially interested in a unity movement based on these documents.

A century and a half earlier, Campbell had stated that the "Christian institution" was divided into five "chapters": faith, worship, morality, philosophy, and tradition. On the first three chapters, he said, there already was agreement among all Christians. The confessions of faith agreed with respect to "the direct testimony of God found in the New Testament concerning himself—concerning his Son and Spirit—concerning mankind—what he has done, and what he will do."[35] He believed that the churches agreed on the second chapter concerning worship. All taught that "God is to be worshipped through the Mediator—in prayer, in praise, public and private—in the ordinances of Christian baptism, the Lord's day, the Lord's supper, and in the study of his word and of his works in creation and providence."[36]

The elements of worship, he later affirmed, were prescribed but not the order, ceremony, or exact words to be spoken, which were left to the judgment of the church. Christ's intent, he insisted, was that the basic act of Sunday worship be "the breaking of the loaf"—the celebration of the Eucharist. He said very little about the third chapter, the moral code. All the churches confessed and acknowledged the same morality, although "in the practice of it there are great subtractions."[37]

The chapters of philosophy and tradition, Campbell continued, had been added by people in later generations and were the cause of the "partyism, vain jangling, and heresies that have disgraced the Christian profession." Examples included doctrines such as "the Son eternally begotten of the Father," the "active and passive obedience of Christ," and "evangelical repentance."[38] Although Campbell was willing for people to hold those ideas privately, he was unwilling for them to be discussed in public meetings of the church.

---

[35] Alexander Campbell, *A Connected View of the Principles and Rules by which the Living Oracles May Be Intelligently and Certainly Interpreted* (Bethany, WV: McVay and Ewing, 1835), 123

[36] Ibid., 124.

[37] Ibid.

[38] Ibid.

My feeling about the COCU documents was that the language in the 1966 *Principles of Church Union* was consistent with tenets of evangelical Christianity as Campbell had described them. I could imagine that had he been a delegate to COCU he would have been able to give his affirmation to that text. Later drafts, however, including the 1970 *Plan of Union,* began to incorporate materials that resembled the philosophies and traditions that Campbell had scorned. He would have found himself among the people whose interest in the united church was waning. The *Plan of Union* also added what Alexander Campbell might have called a sixth chapter—government—and he would undoubtedly have objected to it.

After Memphis, I could see with new clarity that consensus statements such as the *Plan of Union* show the extent to which all the churches believe and practice the one Christian faith. The tragedy and scandal of our long history is that, despite the fact that we hold this gospel in common, we still live separated lives. Even Disciples, with our vocation for Christian unity, continue to live our own ecclesial (dare we say denominational) life and continue to cultivate our own traditions and philosophies.

One more observation should be made about the Memphis convocation and the actions the churches took. Few people other than the immediate participants paid attention to what we did. Whereas in the early years of the Consultation on Church Union, the discussions between the churches were newsworthy, even in major American journals and papers, in these later times, discussions and actions do not bring out the cameras and reporters' notebooks. Declining in membership, with aging constituents, and no longer positioned among the essential institutions in public life, the mainline churches are largely ignored. The question that haunts me during my later years is this: Can the movement toward unity represented by Churches Uniting in Christ lead to the reconstruction of congregational life and the recovery of vitality among mainline churches? During the later phase of my ministry, the vitality of the church has become the most important issue for my continuing theological activity.

Four

Churches of the Third Type

My college, seminary, and graduate studies took place during the post-World War II surge of religion. Long-established congregations were growing at significant rates, and new congregations were being started, especially in the post-war suburbs, with many of them showing rapid growth patterns. It was easy to believe that this return to religion would continue indefinitely and that the Protestant denominations that had already established themselves on Main Street, USA, would become increasingly dominant in American culture. The Christian Church (Disciples of Christ) shared in this surge of energy, as can be seen in many communities across the country where large church buildings were erected following the war in prominent locations.

By 1961, when I began my teaching career at Christian Theological Seminary, however, the mood in American life was changing. The surge of religious life had reached a crest in 1958, and the post-war tide of religious energy began to ebb. Furthermore, the rip tides created by Catholic and evangelical churches were gathering strength as the mainstream Protestant waters subsided. This movement toward a changed religious America reached a new intensity in 1968, one of the most difficult years of the twentieth century, when a cultural revolution in the United States convulsed political and institutional life. My sunny experiences in the liturgical–ecumenical world were overshadowed by the increasingly heavy clouds of the diminishment of mainstream Protestantism, including the Christian Church (Disciples of Christ). Through the years my perplexity has deepened, and this chapter describes my efforts to understand and respond to these changes. Throughout this period, the relationship of eucharistic worship,

Christian worship, and congregational life continued to be a central factor in my work.

Pastoral Beginnings

During my four years at Northwest Christian College (1949–1953), I served the Christian Church in Dayton, Oregon, first as youth associate and then as student pastor. The Pioneer Evangelical United Brethren Church had long been the leading congregation in town, but the Christian Church was gradually taking on that eminence. The Baptist and Assembly of God congregations were struggling to survive. Despite my immaturity, I managed to do my pastoral duties well enough that the congregation held its own. My seminary student pastorate (1953–1956) was with the Christian Church of Somerset, Indiana. This historic but fragile congregation had long vied with the Methodist Church in our village, with the Methodists clearly in the lead when I arrived in the community. In my first fall in Somerset, the congregation's historic church building was destroyed by fire. While rebuilding our church, we met for worship on the stage of the township high school across the street from the parsonage. With a little help from the Disciples Board of Church Extension, the members of the congregation designed a new building, salvaged oak timber from a member's bottom land, and with their own hands built a new church. By the time I completed my ministry, the attendance had increased dramatically; our church received an award as the "rural church of the year" among Disciples in Indiana.

During my seminary years, the mood on campus was in tune with the dramatic growth of religion throughout American life. Dean Shelton presided over a rapidly growing student body, and his optimistic, entrepreneurial spirit shaped life on campus. Much of what the students encountered pointed toward the increasing dominance of Protestant churches in American life. During these years I was thinking through a career decision, choosing between the pastoral ministry and teaching in a theological seminary. Inspired by the example of Ralph Sockman and W. J. Jarman, two of the most memorable lecturers during my seminary years, I chose Pacific School of Religion in Berkeley as the location for doctoral studies, with the intention of being a pastor who would provide intellectual and spiritual leadership in communities where I would later serve.

During the three years between graduation from the School of Religion and my enrollment at Pacific School of Religion, I was pastor of the Christian Church in Sanger, California. I worked hard at my pastoral labors in Sanger, trying to implement the ideas about church organization I had learned from Dean Shelton in my seminary classes. His book, *The Church Functioning Effectively*, which he had published after becoming the seminary's dean, was based on his years of highly successful pastoral leadership in Oklahoma, Texas, and Missouri. One of his presuppositions was that the organization of the congregation, "with leaders responsible for various functions, is firmly rooted in the teachings of the New Testament."[1] His organizational system divided the congregation's life and work into seven functional departments and assigned responsibility for each function to an appointed group of church members. The pastor was consultant to these leaders and administrator of the church as a whole. The pastor was to attend the meetings of all these departments, but their success depended on the commitment and actions of the members of these groups. As best I can recall, I tried to work in Sanger along the lines of Shelton's book.

I also used a book that was published just as I was entering into full-time pastoral work—H. Richard Niebuhr's volume, *The Purpose of the Church and Its Ministry*.[2] Although Niebuhr was an academic theologian, he wrote this book in his capacity as director of the Study of Theological Education in the United States and Canada, sponsored by the American Association of Theological Schools. In this slender volume, Niebuhr described the minister's role with a new title—pastoral director—that was easily misunderstood and therefore easily rejected, but he helped me understand an idea that was implicit in Shelton's approach to leadership in the congregation. Niebuhr affirmed that the leading idea of the time was that the congregation rather than the pastor was the minister in the community. The pastor's primary responsibility was to challenge and

---

[1] Orman L. Shelton, *The Church Functioning Effectively* (St. Louis: Christian Board of Publication, 1946), 23. During Shelton's six years at Ponca City, the church received 1,661 additions and doubled in membership. When he left the Independence Boulevard Christian Church in Kansas City to become the dean at the School of Religion, the congregation's membership was 2,679.

[2] H. Richard Niebuhr, *The Purpose of the Church and Its Ministry* (New York: Harper & Row, 1956).

guide the church to perform its service. I could easily understand myself in this role, although it became clear that my skills in this kind of leadership were undeveloped.

The idea that made the strongest impression upon me, however, was that the near-frantic, busy character of pastoral work was largely the result of confusion in the church and its ministers concerning the central purpose of ministerial work. When ministers knew what they were doing, they would be able "to resist the inner pressures to which [they are] subject from lay groups in the churches, from the society, from denominational headquarters, and from within [themselves]."[3] Even with this insight, however, I felt the pressure of pastoral leadership, and sometimes experienced the anxiety and depression that much later became serious obstacles to effective pastoral activity.

Although my ministry in Somerset had been successful, at the Sanger church I was found wanting. The decision by the board of elders to ask for my resignation and the opportunity of moving to the Bay Area to begin my doctoral work came simultaneously, which allowed me to leave Sanger with dignity although with diminished self-confidence.[4] In contrast with my modest pastoral record at Sanger, some Disciples congregations in California were experiencing solid growth. Dallas Gladson, pastor of First Christian Church, Oakland, told me that he could have 200 new members a year if he had time or staff to follow up on visitors and integrate new members into congregational life. Had I been willing to leave Sanger a year earlier than I did, I could have become that associate minister; for a little while I would have worked with a classic liberal, whose confident spirit and stimulating preaching sustained an active and growing congregation.

It would have been an illuminating and challenging experience to work with a sophisticated urban congregation and to talk through, with my colleague pastor and members of the congregation, the theological issues with which we were dealing—including the nature and meaning of Jesus Christ. I had been reading D. M. Baillie's book on Christology, *God Was in Christ*, in order to find a way to tell

---

[3] Ibid., 55.

[4] The elders reached their decision in a conference with Charles Severns, the regional minister, in the spring of 1959, while I was out of town attending a conference. I began my doctoral studies in September.

people how Jesus was special and why they should pattern their lives according to his teachings and example.[5] Gladson was also interested in preaching about Jesus, but in ways "that made sense to people for whom everything about Easter was an embarrassment."

A year later, when I could move, I became part-time associate minister at Barrett Avenue Christian Church, a new Disciples congregation in Richmond, California. The pastor, Russell Coatney, was a pragmatic, partially liberalized traditionalist, with roots in Texas and Oklahoma. Like Gladson, he conveyed confidence and had well-developed skills in working with the people of his congregation. His preaching, however, dealt more with organizational matters and inspirational encouragement than with the theological and ethical issues that were prominent in Gladson's preaching. The Barrett Avenue Church, where I spent a year and a half as part-time associate minister, had reached the high point of its growth curve and was beginning a decline. Although I assumed that the growing discontent with the pastor's leadership was the primary cause, I later came to realize that at Barrett Avenue we were already seeing the downturn that would soon affect even the churches with strong and confident pastoral leadership.

Midway through my residency for the doctorate at Pacific School of Religion, I was invited to consider teaching church administration and worship at CTS. At that point, I still was intending to be a pastor in the years to come. Because my formal studies were in church history, I initially resisted the CTS offer to teach in the practical field. When it became clear that I could make worship the major partner in my teaching, thus drawing on historical and theological studies as well as practical issues, I accepted the invitation. Shortly before my thirtieth birthday, my family and I moved to Indianapolis so that I could devote the summer to preparations for my first semester of teaching. Summer session was in process, with a large percentage of the students being mature pastors back on campus for further study. At lunch one day, I was talking with one of these men, ten or fifteen years my senior. With considerable disdain in his manner, he asked me if in my few years in the pastorate I had learned enough to teach these experienced men how to do their work. I don't recall my answer, but as I look back on my career teaching pastoral work

---

[5] D. M. Baillie, *God Was in Christ: An Essay on Incarnation and Atonement* (New York: Scribner, 1948).

and church administration, I conclude that I probably never have known enough to teach people what they needed to know.

When we moved to Indianapolis, we quickly chose University Park Christian Church rather than Northwood Christian Church as our church. It was closer to our home, within a not-unreasonable walking distance. With 1,000 members and an average attendance of 325, it was half the size of Northwood but much larger than any congregation with which we had previously been associated. Several seminary colleagues, including Dean Ronald Osborn, were members, as were several of the Disciples' national staff persons, including Gaines Cook, executive of the International Convention, and Hollis Turley, president of the Pension Fund. A small number of Butler University professors were active members, among them Alexander Jones, who later became university president. James Stuart, longtime editor of the *Indianapolis Star*, was still present on most Sundays, despite his frail health. Among the Indianapolis businesspeople in the congregation was Harold Dice, general manager of Allison Division of General Motors and a GM vice president. On many Sundays a young woman who worked in a low-paying job at a Chevrolet plant sat a couple of rows behind him.

Although the membership was, on average, older than my wife, Billie, and I, we were part of a goodly number of families with young children—including two Palmer brothers and their sister, each with four children; the Cowans and Wells, with four each; and the Martzes, with six. The Sunday school had a class of a dozen or more children for each grade in school and junior and senior high programs with a dozen to twenty youth in each.

The pastor, Lowell C. Bryant, was a prominent Disciples leader, congenial, and well organized. His theology was traditional and he communicated well with many people in the congregation blend. Bryant's approach to church management was based on Orman L. Shelton's model, and he managed the system diligently. During our early years in the congregation, the membership remained stable, although the clergy members were increasingly restive (and two of them transferred to Northwood during our early years in Indianapolis). Some of the members remembered the exciting and theologically solid preaching of Bryant's predecessor, and they were aware of the strong music and dramatic preaching at Northwood. As University Park's growth slowed, it was easy to believe that much of the fault could be assigned to the pastor, who seemed increasingly out of step with the mood of the 1960s and the transformation of American society that was taking place. He seemed especially ill-suited to the culturally liberal Butler-Tarkington neighborhood in which the church was located.

One of the reasons I so readily accepted preaching opportunities in other churches, sometimes for months at a time, was that I could be away from my own church in an honorable way. I took an active role in our congregation's program and early in our Indianapolis sojourn organized and directed a Sunday evening school for Christian living, with 165 people in attendance. Our pastor had been trying unsuccessfully for several years to set up the program and was overjoyed when we finally had one.

Following the completion of my first six years at the seminary, I was eligible for a research leave and was called to be visiting minister-theologian at University Christian Church in Seattle, where Robert A. Thomas was pastor. Here, the decline of membership that was just beginning in Indianapolis was already far advanced. Thomas had succeeded John Paul Pack, who, like Dallas Gladson of Oakland, was a warm often exciting preacher. Pack's sermons, which I received through the mail during my college years, were based on a simple idea—that life makes the kind of sense that Jesus said it does. Thomas told me that Pack's approach to church life had been to invite everyone, regardless of their theology and predilections into membership, and to keep these people in little groups separated from one another. On this basis, which sounds much like the approach of contemporary megachurches, it was possible to attract a large and theologically diverse congregation.

Thomas's approach, in contrast, was to speak an aggressively liberal and transformative message, knowing that many people would find it unacceptable. As they left, he was convinced, many others would come, especially people from the university community. His leadership was undermined by the fact that the people he expected to attract did not come. Many people were dropping out of church, and those who stayed were swarming to University Presbyterian and University Congregational. Although these two churches were quite different from each other in their theologies, their stance toward the larger community was more like Pack's than Thomas's. I found Thomas's preaching exciting, and Sunday after

Sunday I experienced a sense of rising excitement as sermon time approached. The congregation's music was strong and, in general, life at University Christian Church was invigorating.

Although the Seattle congregation seemed to be well-adapted to contemporary American life, especially in comparison with our Indianapolis congregation, it was declining much more rapidly. One reason was that Seattle and the University of Washington experienced the tumult of the Vietnam era earlier and more intensely than did Indianapolis and Butler University. Another reason was that Robert Thomas rushed eagerly forward into the turmoil, to the distress of many members of the congregation, whereas Lowell Bryant resisted the distress and tried to shield his congregation from its terrors.

What I was experiencing in these two congregations was taking place in a large percentage of mainline Protestant churches. Some were dwindling with little apparent cause. Ray Montgomery, who had been the longtime pastor of Speedway Christian Church in Indianapolis, told one of my classes that, whereas before Vietnam he could count on 200 new members a year, now the number was greatly reduced. He was less troubled, however, by the diminished number of new members than by the fact that longtime members, for no apparent reason, were simply disappearing. They weren't leaving town and, as far as he could tell, they weren't mad. They simply were dropping out, and he didn't know how to respond. Other congregations, however, were torn apart by what we later came to call culture wars. Some writers of the time, like Jeffrey Hadden, claimed that the reason was that activist pastors forced their congregations to face the troubling issues in American life only to find that the congregations broke apart and that the pastors were out of work.[6]

Professor of Church Administration and Worship

While I was beginning to confront the decline of mainline churches, both in my personal experience as a churchgoer and in my reading, I was also teaching classes according to a more conventional understanding of pastoral leadership. During my early years, I read

---

[6] Jeffrey K. Hadden, *The Gathering Storm in the Churches* (Garden City, NY: Doubleday, 1969).

widely in practical writings dealing with organizational leadership.⁷ Some of these readings confirmed the things I had previously learned from teachers like Shelton, and others helped me understand new approaches to leadership. Two books illustrate the way I was approaching my work as professor of church administration. The first was Douglas McGregor's book, *The Human Side of Enterprise*, in which he contrasted two kinds of organization—X and Y.⁸ McGregor helped me think about motivations of church people for doing their work, and this line of thought began the process of undercutting my confidence in the functional church organization.

A second book that influenced my early years of teaching church administration was Peter Drucker's *The Effective Executive*, which provided a way to develop one of the insights I had found in Niebuhr's book on ministry.⁹ Drucker stated that executives—and here I substituted pastors—were always pressured by the demands of their organizations. Three keys to effective leadership I gleaned from the book were these: An effective minister concentrates on those tasks that only a person in the minister's position can achieve, gives primary attention to those tasks that make the greatest difference in the church's well-being, and protects significant blocks of time to accomplish major tasks. Although these guidelines would not remove the demands, pastors who followed them would be able to decide which things to do and which to leave undone.

I supplemented my reading with conversations with pastors of churches, especially in Indianapolis—people like Elbert Cole of North United Methodist Church, Harley Patterson of Central Christian Church, Richard Hamilton of St. Luke's United Methodist Church, David Bobo of Fountain Square Church of Christ, and Paul

---

⁷ Although Beauford Norris had taught church administration for a couple of years, my real predecessor was Orman L. Shelton. As I look back, I am aware of the remarkable contrast. He came to his work at the high point of his career, after serving congregations with as many as 2,000 members. I came as a graduate student who had been fired from his only full-time pastorate. Although Shelton may have read in the field of organizational development, his primary base was his own successful experience. I had to depend on my reading and my ability to adapt organizational theory to the work of pastors.

⁸ Douglas McGregor, *The Human Side of Enterprise* (New York: McGraw-Hill, 1960).

⁹ Peter Drucker, *The Effective Executive* (New York: Harper & Row, 1966, 1967).

Stauffer of Northwood Christian Church. Cole's approach to his work at a large, demanding congregation seemed a perfect illustration of Drucker's principles. His church leaders and he agreed that his most important work at North Church was to conduct inspiring worship and to preach strong sermons; the corollary was that he had to arrange his time to fulfill that expectation. He knew that every week he had to devote about twenty hours, including two or three blocks of time, each of them three or four hours long, to this task. Every week, therefore, he scheduled in those blocks of time between the appointments and meetings that he had agreed to.

In my classes on church administration, I tried to help students develop a methodology for effective pastoral leadership, but my efforts were undermined by two questions that were forcing themselves on the attention of church leaders everywhere: Why were Protestant churches declining, and how could pastors lead their congregations to new vitality and effectiveness? The first question was answered for me by Langdon Gilkey in his book, *How the Church Can Minister to the World Without Losing Itself*.[10] The other half of my teaching responsibility—Christian worship—provided answers to the second.

Gilkey's premise was that the church, "if it is to be itself and do its work, must mediate to the world some Word, some Presence, some norm and standard, that are both transcendent in their origin—in some measure 'holy'—and also relevant to the world."[11] He showed that the Roman Catholic Church and conservative Protestant churches, although starting from opposite compass points, had come to much the same place. Each had maintained strong connections with the holy, although in ways that had little relevance to the secular world. For Catholics, the "separated, holy elements are the controlling apostolic clergy, the sacraments, canon law, the dogmas, and the monastic orders."[12] For conservative Protestants, these elements are "biblical doctrines which nothing can question, … the vivid emotional experience of salvation, which every believer should experience, and … the moral code of personal freedom from vice."[13] In contrast, liberal Protestant churches had embraced the thought patterns and values of the secular world but

---

[10] Langdon Gilkey, *How the Church Can Minister to the World Without Losing Itself* (New York: Harper & Row, 1964).
[11] Ibid., 2.
[12] Ibid., 5.
[13] Ibid., 44.

had lost their contact with the holy, except for their determination to establish justice in human affairs. Liberalism, Gilkey said, had "reinterpreted Christianity, its gospel, and its ethics" in the terms of scientific method and contemporary culture, and thus had "made Christianity into the religious expression of this developing scientific and humanitarian culture."[14] Gilkey's diagnosis helped explain my church experiences. A few people were leaving angrily because their churches were attacking major aspects of the very culture the churches were trying to legitimate. A larger number, however, were drifting away from mainstream churches because preaching, worship, and church life no longer connected them to religious power, and the secular reasons for church attendance that were its substitutes no longer held them.

Gilkey was convinced that liberal Protestantism could recover its vitality and continue as the dominant religious force in American culture, and he proposed that three biblical figures showed the way for liberal Protestant churches to go. The symbol "people of God" pointed to the church's calling to be a new community, bound together by God's Spirit, and committed to being a place for reconciling people and the churches.[15] The symbol "hearers of the Word" pointed to the presence of Jesus Christ as the living Word of God within the church, witnessed to by the Bible, proclaimed by the pastor, and experienced by the people as life-changing truth. The symbol "Body of Christ" pointed to the numinous experience of receiving the "judgment and the loving mercy of God ... in the most direct and real manner possible."[16] When I reread Gilkey's book, thirty-five years after its publication, I could see that his diagnosis of our condition had impacted my work more than his prescription for a cure. Although I have often used his diagnostic ideas, I did not remember the three chapters in which he discussed the symbols that could lead to the renewal of liberal Protestantism.

What perplexes me especially is the fact that while most of the book is copiously marked, from at least two readings in my early years of teaching, the chapter on the sacraments is almost unmarked. The chapter that dealt directly and seriously with my own area of interest made little impact on me.

---

[14] Ibid., 47.
[15] Ibid., 73.
[16] Ibid., 121.

Although I seemed to have overlooked this part of Gilkey's discussion, I was focusing attention on worship as a way to help mainline churches move through the crisis that was developing around them. Three short monographs I wrote during the late 1960s indicate what I was thinking at the time. The first is an unpublished manuscript that I titled, "The Impossibility and the Possibility of Worship." It is carefully typed, with footnotes, but no date. Most of the references are to publications with dates in the late 1950s and early 1960s, with the latest citations from periodicals in 1965. I presume that I did the first draft during the summer of 1965 and revised it during the next school year. One of the seminary's special lecturers was H. Grady Davis, a Lutheran professor of preaching whose book had impressed me greatly. Davis was one of the editors of a series of slender monographs being published by SCM Press in England and John Knox Press in the United States, with the general title, "Ecumenical Studies in Worship." I discussed the manuscript with Davis, who indicated an interest in seeing it, probably because he liked the selection of psalms from the Revised Standard Version I had prepared for use in Sweeney Chapel.[17] I remember revising the manuscript and arranging to have it typed in good form. After many months with no word from Davis, I wrote to him for a progress report. He responded with a few lines indicating that the manuscript was not suited to the series.

I made no other effort to have the manuscript published. Perhaps Davis's rejection confirmed what I already sensed—that the manuscript was not yet ready for wider distribution. I probably used some of the ideas in classes, however. Reading the manuscript now, I recognize its serious limitations and am relieved that I made no further effort to publish this eighty-page working paper. It was my first serious effort to describe the "mood of our time," the tendency to understand life without reference to God. I acknowledged that conventional worship in Protestant churches was problematic, but I also stated that efforts to continue worship as a celebration of human life, without reference to God, would also fail. I was convinced, however, that despite the challenges faced by the churches, the worship of God would continue. I asserted that the natural world

---

[17] This selection was incorporated into *Hymnbook for Christian Worship*, Charles Huddleston Heaton (ed.) (St. Louis: Bethany Press, 1970).

and human nature continued unchanged even while the technical language we used to describe them was changing rapidly.

One reason I never went back to this manuscript is that the book I wrote in 1968, while on leave at Seattle's University Christian Church, became a more mature expression of many of the same ideas.[18] Using materials I had been working on throughout the year, I completed this manuscript during the weeks between the assassinations of Martin Luther King Jr. and Robert Kennedy—and the emotions I felt during that turbulent year bleed through the pages of the book. By this time, I had read extensively from books and essays by Ernst Cassirer and Susanne K. Langer, and I was beginning to understand their "philosophy of symbolic forms." Following their lead, I described worship as high art that expresses the deepest values of the Christian community and implants them in the lives of worshipers. After giving examples of the bleak understanding of life that I perceived in popular culture, I reaffirmed the vision of reality that comes to its embodiment in Jesus of Nazareth. Again with Langer in mind, I interpreted this vision as tragic in character, consistent with Jesus' statement that "he who finds his life will lose it, and he who loses his life for my sake will find it" (Matthew 10:39).[19] In order to discuss the conflict in many churches over traditional forms of worship and changes that were crowding in on the church, I discussed the relationship between feeling and form in worship, drawing on Langer's understanding of the way that each depends on the other.

The conclusion to this part of the book is a chapter in which I discussed four characteristics I believed to be necessary: The mood of worship would be the sense of tragic rejoicing as worshipers contemplated God's work for us in the suffering and exaltation of Jesus Christ. Worship would translate this gospel into forms from

---

[18] Keith Watkins, *Liturgies in a Time When Cities Burn* (Nashville, TN: Abingdon Press, 1969).

[19] Ibid., 43. I used four of Susanne K. Langer's books: *Philosophy in a New Key: A Study in the Symbolism of Reason, Rite and Art* (New York: A Mentor Book, 1951); *Feeling and Form: A Theory of Art Developed from Philosophy in a New Key* (New York: Charles Scribner's Sons, 1953); *Philosophical Sketches: A Study of the Human Mind in Relation to Feeling, Explored through Art, Language, and Symbol* (New York: A Mentor Book, 1964); and *Reflections on Art: A Source Book of Writings by Artists, Critics, and Philosophers,* edited by Susanne K. Langer (New York: A Galaxy Book, 1961).

contemporary life. It would lead irresistibly to serving people in the world. Worship would direct worshipers to the source of strength—the God who raised Jesus from the dead. In the next two chapters, I dealt with major elements in liturgical structure. One of them presented principles that would shape worship in the free tradition, and the second discussed the calendar, both the weekly pattern of worship and the calendar of the Christian year. Then came a chapter, describing my work in Seattle, that was intended to be a model of how wise pastoral leaders could bring about change along these lines.

After *Liturgies* was published, I realized that the title implied that the book would present liturgies for the difficult times in which we were living—for times of riot and bloodshed, protest, grief, and hope. The book would have been much stronger if one chapter had discussed principles for developing these alternative liturgies. The book was deficient in its failure to discuss initiation, especially the transmission of faith to adults who were turning to the church for hope in times of terrible distress. The book did include an appendix with prayers for use at the communion table, based in part on laments from Isaiah: "Today we cry to you. In the cities of our land little children die for want of food, and strong men search for work. Neighborhoods decay while urban sprawl despoils the countryside. ... Send forth your Word and Presence that we may be healed."[20] I remember reading one of these prayers in a meeting at the church in Seattle and, to my great surprise, one of the young women in the meeting laughed at the silly language. Reading these prayers thirty years later, however, I find my tragic mode confirmed by eucharistic prayers drafted in more recent years by Roman Catholic theologian David N. Power. In an extended text, designed for use in Roman Catholic liturgies, Power includes this paragraph:

> Calling to mind your love, it is a cross that we remember.
> In the weak and humbled flesh of your child, Jesus,
> we acknowledge your presence upon this earth.
> In his wounds, we see you afflicted with all our wounds.
> In his unjust sentencing, we see you condemned
> with all those who have no power.

---

[20] Ibid., 162–163.

But in his death, we see you shattering death and its dominion.

For this, we praise you and give you thanks.[21]

In the last twenty-five pages of *Liturgies*, I discussed two topics that are closely connected to the liturgical exposition that takes up most of the book. The one that is especially interesting to me as I look back on it is the conclusion that three kinds of Protestantism that were available to us. Evangelical Protestantism and liberal Protestantism were presented briefly as parallel efforts to continue theologies, lifestyles, and congregational life from an earlier generation into our own time. I indicated that each one had certain strengths and notable weaknesses, so that neither could be an adequate option for the future. Instead, we needed what I called "a third type of Protestantism," which would be "more determined than … liberal Protestantism to represent the major tradition of Christianity [and] more committed than evangelical Protestantism to communicate with people who have lost contact with the Bible, traditional theology, and clearly recognized religious experience." This third type, I continued, united "the catholic-reformed-evangelical streams of classical Christian tradition." It had "a tough-mindedness about the needs of contemporary life, dealing rigorously and often unconventionally with questions of faith and ethics."[22]

I realized that it would be difficult for churches of the third type to flourish, because they would require significant changes in church life and because the population of church-going people was sure to diminish. These congregations, I insisted, needed to embrace both people who were already attuned to this new style of church and others who were more conventional in their attitudes and ideas. In these mixed congregations, I proposed, "the new style must establish the tone and point the direction of advance. Yet it must do so in such a way as to utilize folkways that represent catholicity, for they are the conveyer, the means of communication that bring the people toward the new style."[23]

---

[21] David N. Power, "The Eucharistic Prayer: Another Look." In Frank C. Senn (ed.), *New Eucharistic Prayers: An Ecumenical Study of their Development and Structure* (Mahwah, NY: Paulist Press, 1987), 252.

[22] Keith Watkins, *Liturgies in a Time When Cities Burn*, 132.

[23] Ibid., 143.

The Reshaping of American Church Life

Even though I acknowledged that this third kind of Protestantism would be difficult to bring into prominence, I had seriously underestimated the impact of the revolt of the next two decades, which Robert Wuthnow encapsulated in the title of a book: *The Restructuring of American Religion*.[24] When we came back from our year in Seattle, I could see changes happening in the churches of Indianapolis, especially in the pre-World War II suburbs around Butler, the seminary, and our home. These neighborhoods had been among the most desirable residential sections of the city, and they were graced with strong Roman Catholic and Protestant congregations, most of which had grown rapidly during the post-war return to religion.

By 1970, however, changes were taking place. After an initial period of stress because of the movement northward of African American residents, these neighborhoods settled into a stable period of racial integration and continuity of neighborhood institutions. Two of the elementary schools serving the community reflected the changing demographics of the community and maintained their longtime reputation as high-performance places. For the most part, however, the churches in the community continued to be essentially one-race congregations and lost membership and institutional strength. Congregations that had been flagship churches for their communions, such as Meridian Street United Methodist and First-Meridian Heights Presbyterian, surrendered that eminence to congregations in newer suburbs, especially St. Luke United Methodist and Second Presbyterian. In these new communities on the far north side of the city, some congregations flourished while others never moved out of plateaus reached soon after their establishment. Some congregations, including Trader's Point Christian and Ninety-First Street Christian (both affiliated with the Christian Churches and Churches of Christ), and Devonshire Baptist Church became megachurches.

The one Disciples congregation to show dramatic growth was an African American congregation that in 1960 (as Second Christian Church) had a membership of 781 and in 1995 (as Light of the World

---

[24] Robert Wuthnow, *The Restructuring of American Religion: Society and Faith Since World War II* (Princeton, NJ: Princeton University Press, 1988).

Christian Church) reported 2,336 members. Although Assemblies of God and Nazarene Churches did not develop megachurches in this part of the city during my years in Indianapolis, the Church of God (Anderson) developed a strong congregation. One of the Roman Catholic congregations in the older neighborhood—St. Joan of Arc—declined significantly, but at the same time St. Thomas Aquinas flourished. My impression was that the two Episcopal churches in the urban neighborhoods—Trinity and St. Paul's—maintained themselves at much the same level they had attained earlier, but that the two Lutheran congregations—Our Redeemer and Bethlehem—struggled to maintain their strength.

Especially unsettling to me was the decline of Disciples in comparison with United Methodists. When we first moved to Indianapolis, five north-side United Methodist churches (Broad Ripple, Broadway, Meridian Street, North, and St. Luke) reported a combined membership of 9,961. The corresponding Disciples congregations (Broad Ripple-Allisonville, Third, Northwood, University Park, and Williams Creek-Crestview) reported 5,069—51 percent of the Methodist total. In 1995, when I retired and moved to Arizona, those same United Methodist congregations had declined by 61 percent, to 3,977 members, and Disciples had lost 69 percent, down to 1,580 members—now only 40 percent of the Methodist total. Further north, United Methodist congregations in Castleton, Carmel and Fishers grew rapidly, while the Disciples' Carmel Christian Church struggled throughout this period. Only the Geist Christian Church, founded in 1985, was able to grow at a steady rate.[25]

In his study of religion in Indiana, from which I gathered these statistics, L. C. Rudolph also discovered the dramatic shift that had

---

[25] I can illustrate the shift by comparing the changes in several congregations that can be arranged in pairs. Even in 1958, when Disciples were at a high point in their strength, United Methodists were doing even better: Broad Ripple United Methodist, 1,044, compared with Broad Ripple (later Allisonville) Christian, 508; Meridian Street United Methodist, 2,158, compared with Northwood Christian, 1,675; North United Methodist, 2,955, compared with University Park Christian, 1,075; St. Luke United Methodist, 473, compared with Williams Creek (later Crestwood) Christian, 148; Broadway United Methodist, 3,331, compared with Third Christian, 1,709. In 1995, the pairs reported these figures: Broad Ripple United Methodist, 333, compared with Allisonville Christian, 345; Broadway United Methodist, 436, compared with Third Christian, 330; Meridian Street United Methodist, 1,845, compared with Northwood, 561; St. Luke, 2,110, compared with Crestview, 210.

taken place in the relative strength of the three branches of the Christian Church movement. In 1925, when the College of Religion began its work at Butler University, the Disciples of Christ *Yearbook* listed 706 congregations in Indiana, with a total membership of 139,989 in participating churches and 37,525 in nonparticipating churches. By 1990, the picture had changed dramatically. According to Rudolph's summary, the conservative branch, called Churches of Christ, reported 39,953 adherents. The Christian Church (Disciples of Christ), which Rudolph described as the "more liberal, ecumenical, and mainline denomination," reported 89,932 adherents. Rudolph referred to "a center segment of the Christians in Indiana, and the third largest denomination in the state, with 160,099 adherents."[26]

Disciples also lost ground elsewhere in the United States, with Los Angeles County an especially clear example. A study of sixty-seven congregations that were present throughout the period from 1921 through 1981 indicates that, from 1921 through 1929, their membership increased from 6,000 to 15,000. After holding steady for a decade, they experienced another spurt from 1938 through 1959, rising to 32,000 members. From 1964 through 1981, however, membership fell precipitously, from 31,000 to 19,000. In cities throughout Southern California, such as Pomona, rapidly growing congregations erected impressive new and large buildings in the years just after World War II. Scarcely had these buildings been constructed when membership plummeted. The same Dallas Gladson who had confidently spoken of 200 new members a year in Oakland during the mid-1950s, moved to Whittier's First Christian Church and watched membership fall from its high point of 2,285 members in 1958 to 1,530 members in 1967. The congregation continued to shrink, falling to 705 at the time of the 1981 study.[27] Similar collapses took place in other cities and denominations. In Springfield, Massachusetts, for example, the long-dominant United Church of Christ lost nearly half of its membership between 1965 and 1975.[28]

---

[26] L. C. Rudolph, *Hoosier Faiths: A History of Indiana Churches & Religious Groups* (Bloomington, IN: Indiana University Press, 1995), 60.

[27] Michael C. Wolfe, "The Growth and Decline of the Christian Church (Disciples of Christ) in Los Angeles County: What Could Our Future Be?" Unpublished professional project, Claremont School of Theology, 1983.

[28] This dramatic decline was stated by N. J. Demerath III and Rhys H. Williams in *A Bridging of Faiths: Religion and Politics in a New England City* (Princeton, NJ: Princeton University Press, 1992), 38.

In Indianapolis, most congregations that lost membership were located in portions of the city that had been built prior to World War II or soon thereafter. Nearly all of them were mainline Protestant and Catholic churches. Despite the diminishment of the mainline churches, evangelical churches did not rush in to take up the slack. What happened to the people who had attended these large congregations? Some transferred out to congregations further north. Others moved out and were replaced by people with less interest in churches. Still others stayed in their old neighborhoods but stopped going to church. Nearly all congregations that grew rapidly were on the high-growth, newly developing edges of the city. This is where the evangelical megachurches were able to thrive, as did some mainline churches, such as Second Presbyterian and St. Luke United Methodist. Other mainline churches in similar far-north-side locations, however, barely held their own or lost ground. For me, the difficult puzzle was why Disciples were so impotent.

As an active Christian and church member, and as a seminary professor, I was continually pushed to understand these developments and to suggest ways for churches like mine and students in our seminary to respond. One of the many books that discussed the changes in the American religious scene was especially helpful to me: *Understanding Church Growth and Decline*.[29] The editors compiled a portfolio of sociological studies describing and analyzing the dramatic changes that had occurred in mainline churches over the previous two decades. I liked the book because it presented a broad array of facts from a wide range of churches and theological perspectives. Although it presented several theories about the changes, one explanation often disagreed with another. I read the book thoroughly, made notations all the way through, and used it in my classes at the seminary for several years.

Several ideas from the book were incorporated into my point of view concerning the changes that were taking place in American life, and I added a few ideas from other sources. The most useful contribution of this book for my reflections was an analytical framework with four elements: national contextual factors, national institutional factors, local contextual factors, and local institutional factors. The social scientists in the book gave slightly greater

---

[29] Dean R. Hoge and David A. Roozen, *Understanding Church Growth and Decline, 1958–1978* (New York/Philadelphia: The Pilgrim Press, 1979).

importance nationally to contextual factors over institutional and on the local level to institutional factors over contextual. Because the decline of mainline churches was so widespread, the primary causes had to be national rather than local. The studies indicated that declines were greatest among the churches that were deeply embedded in mainstream American culture. Growth was most likely to occur in communities of relative affluence and positive demographic change, especially when families with young children were increasing. When these conditions were absent, churches tended to decline. These conclusions provided the general framework that seemed to account for many of the changes I was seeing in Indianapolis.

Because Disciples were declining all over the country, much of their distress could be explained in the same way as that which was experienced by the Presbyterian Church and the United Church of Christ. Yet, Disciples were suffering more serious decline than were other mainline churches, which led to the conclusion that institutional factors within the Disciples intensified the impact of national contextual factors on them. Although none of the essays in the book focused specifically on Disciples, I developed my own notions about the factors that were unique to our churches.

Perhaps the simplest way to state the Disciples' problem, as I thought about these things, was that we had lost faith in the vision that formerly had energized our life and had not found a way to reform, renew, or replace that vision. Disciples' identity, as we understood ourselves and as others perceived us, had always been connected to a specific combination of ideas—communion every Sunday, adult baptism by immersion, the lay eldership, extemporaneous prayer—all based on the assertion that these ideas and these alone were the biblically warranted way for people to receive new life in Christ, organize their churches, and witness to the importance of Christian unity. The more Disciples became culturally conditioned, however, the less persuasive this vision seemed to be. Our modern understanding of the Bible undermined our claim for the authority of our sacramental and ecclesial ideas. The use of biblical language concerning sin and salvation through the blood of Christ became less common among us, with the result that our celebration of the Lord's supper lost much of its religious depth. Although we continued to practice baptism in our traditional fashion, we were more likely to do it that way because this was our tradition rather than because we believed that the mode of baptism was a life-and-death matter. We no longer expected the other churches to become like us as together we sought to find Christian unity.

The loss of our central vision weakened our motivation to preach the gospel, lead people to transformation in Christ, and teach people how to live out their faith in a challenging world. Although I would not have been able to support my hunch, I sensed that the Methodist vision was less subject to damage in its encounter with contemporary culture and that a similar claim could be made of Presbyterian, Lutheran, and Episcopal visions. To use a different metaphor, the Disciples' immune system was more seriously compromised by our contact with contemporary culture, which left us more vulnerable to the debilitating illness of cultural accommodation.

The authors in *Understanding Church Growth and Decline* did not say that external factors were all-powerful. They assumed that institutional factors, especially at the local level, could lead congregations to grow despite the negative pressure of external factors in their communities and nationally. In a chapter described as "commentary," Dean M. Kelley challenged the assumption of the authors in the book that culture is the dominant force, shaping beliefs, value systems, and ways of life. He countered with the statement that it has often been the other way around: "In fact, rather than being victims of changes in cultural climate, religious movements or emphases have often determined, or modified the cultural climate themselves."[30] Kelley proposed that mainline churches had become dependent variables. "When set in a propitiously affluent neighborhood, with the right age, sex, and race mix (or nonmix), it will prosper, but change one or two of the environmental factors a little and it will wane and wither."[31] Kelley was confident that churches did not have to be dependent variables, and he concluded his essay with a powerful challenge: If mainline churches were to take their faith seriously and not allow themselves to be blown around by every cultural change,

---

[30] Dean M. Kelley, "Is Religion a Dependent Variable?" In Dean R. Hoge and David A. Roozen (eds.), *Understanding Church Growth and Decline, 1950 to 1978* (Cleveland: The Pilgrim Press, 1979), 337.

[31] Ibid., 338.

they might begin once again to affect the cultural climate. "They might, in fact, cease to be a dependent and become an independent variable.[32]

Although I was persuaded by Kelley's analysis, I needed examples of congregations that were challenging their cultural setting and, in the process, finding new life for their communities and for themselves. Several were provided by Robert L. Burt, general secretary of the Division of Evangelism and Local Church Development of the United Church of Christ's Division of Homeland Ministries, in a book of case studies of congregations that had found ways of recovering the dynamic for growth.[33] The congregations ranged across a wide spectrum of size and type and were set in different kinds of communities in several sections of the United States. Most of them were long-established churches that had declined and then found a source of new life that resulted in significant transformation and growth.

I used the book in classes in order to encourage students, most of whom were working in congregations in decline. My intention was not that students imitate these pastors but instead learn from them. As they read assigned chapters from the book, they were to ask these questions: (1) What was the situation when the pastor came onto the scene? (2) How did this pastor analyze, assess, and evaluate it? (3) What was the central core of the pastor's leadership? (4) What generalizations can be made as a result?

What these success stories had in common was that a pastor and the people of a congregation generated a new set of local institutional factors that were powerful enough to offset and overcome the general factors that, by themselves, would cause continued decline. In every case, at least two elements were present in this new set of local factors. Together, the pastor and people found a new way of presenting the basic religious message of the church. Frequently, the writers talked about renewal of worship and the recovery of a strong teaching ministry within the congregation. These congregations also developed new momentum in the organizational aspects of their life, reconstructed old buildings or raised new ones, and reestablished basic programs such as evangelism. Little is said in these essays

---

[32] Ibid., 343.
[33] Robert L. Burt (ed.), *Good News in Growing Churches* (Cleveland: The Pilgrim Press, 1992).

about denominational message; rather, these congregations came to renewed vigor by emphasizing the basic elements of the gospel and congregational life. They did these things, however, in ways that were consistent with their long-standing character within mainstream American church life. My hope was that students would find in these stories a way to take heart and assert a bold leadership in their congregations, convinced that whatever might happen to denominations as a whole, their churches could be vital places where people found new life.

I was especially interested in the ideas of a United Methodist pastor enrolled in the doctor of ministry program who had become skilled in taking declining congregations and turning them around. His assessment was that in most of these congregations the necessary elements of church life were present, but the system as a whole was out of synchronization. His task was to reestablish the synchronization. One of his ideas that interested me was that "a modified liturgical form of worship," to use his phrase, was a key element to recovery in these churches. His district superintendent and leaders of the church to which he was assigned would agree that he could consult with them in advance of his transfer, so that on his first Sunday the revised order of worship would be in place. It was important, he believed, that the congregants discover from the first Sunday that there would be a new way of doing things. His proactive approach to leadership extended to other aspects of the congregation's life as he sought to get the entire congregational system back into synchronization. The result was that it scarcely mattered what was happening to Methodists elsewhere.

Proactive leadership, however, is highly demanding, and most people lose their energy or imagination and can no longer stay in front. Even though proactivity may be needed to reestablish synchrony, a different kind of leadership needs to develop as things begin to work effectively. Two books helped me think about these matters, and the response of students in both the M.Div. and the D.Min. programs was usually enthusiastic. D.Min. students were especially positive in their evaluations of John L. Harris's book, *Stress, Power, and Ministry*.[34] Harris believed that many ministers

---

[34] John C. Harris, *Stress, Power, and Ministry: An Approach to the Current Dilemmas of Pastors and Congregations* (Washington, DC: The Alban Institute, 1977).

were afraid because they found themselves in such vulnerable situations; he analyzed the reasons for that fear and proposed ways for pastors to transform their situations, thus neutralizing their fear. He distinguished between four types of leadership—proactive, integrative, reactive, and inactive. The one he recommended for most people most of the time was integrative, in which the pastor and the people learned to work together to achieve goals they could hold in common. One of the corollaries to integrative leadership was that the people and the pastor would all be free to state their convictions and their doubts. They could agree and disagree, yet they could continue working together for the broad purposes of the gospel and the church.

I liked the phrasing by James D. Anderson and Ezra Earl Jones: The goal of leadership in churches is to "forge consensus" rather than to search for "an amenable, smoothed-over, majority point of view." The purpose for this leadership is "faith development." It is "to move from a faith dependent upon others through a process of personal search and exploration to a faith that is owned—integral to self-identity and freely chosen personal values."[35] As director of continuing education at the seminary, I invited Jones to the campus for a continuing education program. He drew a good attendance and presented an elegant analysis of how pastors could move forward effectively.

Despite my efforts to encourage students to develop the kind of leadership that would help their churches become independent variables, the evidence is clear that only a few were able to achieve these results. Consistently, graduates responded to questionnaires by saying that they were least well prepared by seminary studies in the practical skills of ministry. While their biblical studies and systematic theology served them well, their courses in Christian ministries had left them ill-prepared to run a church. I was confident that one reason the classical disciplines fared well and the practical disciplines did not was that there are few practical tests of one's theology and use of the Bible, but the practice of ministry is tested every time attendance and the offering are counted. Indeed, it may be that if students had learned a different theology and approach to the

---

[35] James D. Anderson and Ezra Earl Jones, *The Management of Ministry: Leadership, Purpose, Structure, Community* (San Francisco: Harper & Row, 1978), 59, 131.

Bible, they would have been able to inspire stronger Christians and more vital congregations. Even if that idea could have been proved, however, I had already accepted within myself a significant degree of responsibility for the poor showing of our practical courses.

Taking Lessons from New Teachers

One way to deal with my sense of incapacity was to learn what I could from churches that were growing rapidly while churches like mine were declining. Some writers, like Carl F. George, were connected with the church growth movement emanating from Fuller Theological Seminary.[36] Several books reported on innovative churches, such as the Willow Creek Church in the Midwest and Saddleback Community Church in Southern California. I was especially interested in books like Charles L. Chaney's *Church Planting at the End of the Twentieth Century*, because they proposed ways of adapting one's methods to meet new cultural challenges while continuing to present a message consistent with one's tradition.[37] As I read these books, I recognized certain characteristics in most of the examples: strong leaders who were highly motivated by their understanding of the gospel, a deliberate effort to shape their presentation of the gospel to the particular needs and expectations of a chosen community, a rapidly expanding cohort of people who were being attracted to this fresh presentation of the gospel and were willing to commit their energy to the new venture, and a sharply focused marketing plan that communicated the message in the chosen community. Frequently, these ventures were entrepreneurial start-ups with little financial backing from the outside.

Most of this literature was written by evangelical leaders, and the congregations were usually rapidly growing evangelical churches. Yet, these books often made the point that vital congregations with high-growth potential could be started by people from many faith traditions. Early in his book, Chaney stated that most communities

---

[36] For several years I used one of George's books on administration in classes at the seminary: Carl F. George, *Leading and Managing Your Church* (Old Tappen, NJ: Revell, 1987).

[37] Charles L. Chaney, *Church Planting at the End of the Twentieth Century* (Wheaton, IL: Tyndale House, 1991). Chaney had developed his ideas over an extended period of time during which he had led Southern Baptists in their explosive growth throughout the Midwest and other sections of the country where they had previously had little presence.

have pockets of unchurched people, often as many as 80 percent of the population. "This field," he concluded, "is wide open to Southern Baptists, Methodists, Pentecostals, Lutherans, or any other denomination that will take finding the lost seriously."[38]

A similar point of view was stated even more vigorously by George Barna in a book entitled, *User Friendly Churches: What Christians Need to Know About the Churches People Love to Go to*.[39] Both on the jacket and on the title page, the author described what he meant for a church to be user friendly: "It means providing people with an accessible way to worship God, a comfortable place to bring their friends, and a sensitive, creative community they can belong to—one that is wise enough not to get in the way of the task at hand: reaching the world for Christ." Barna's book was based on his studies of congregations from all parts of the United States, with many different theological, liturgical, and cultural characteristics, and ranging in average worship attendance from 200 to 58,000. It was critical, he noted, to "encompass such a wide array of churches" that readers would be exposed to "principles that transcend the finite limitations of denomination, location, size and theological bent."[40] Barna was especially sensitive to the danger of imitation. No matter how successful a model might be, it could not be transferred to other situations where the leaders, message, and community were different. He believed, however, that principles could be derived from these churches, all of which were marked by two characteristics: worship attendance was growing by at least 10 percent per year, and there was convincing evidence that people were growing spiritually.

In order to provide an experiential base to this reading, I registered for a weekend training program sponsored by Perimeter Presbyterian Church in Atlanta, one of the most striking models of new church development. The congregation had been started in 1977, and nearly two decades later, the organizing pastor was still the central figure in a program of church development that had grown to include eight congregations. The annual workshop for pastors and other church leaders was built around a weekend conference for prospective members, so that we met other pastors who were

---

[38] Ibid., 5.
[39] George Barna, *User Friendly Churches: What Christians Need to Know About the Churches People Love to Go to* (Ventura, CA: Regal Books, 1991).
[40] Ibid. 22.

interested in the Perimeter model, people from the Perimeter staff, and people from Atlanta who were considering membership in this church. We participated in a special program for seekers on Saturday evening and in the regular Sunday services and activities. As has been the case in most of the new churches that have achieved significant growth, Perimeter has been marked by worship that uses contemporary gospel music, small groups as the basic way of helping members develop depth in their Christian life, theology and ministry based on personal transformation through faith in God, and belief in the inerrancy of the Bible and traditional theology.

My experience at Perimeter helped me focus the question that had begun to form as I read the writings of my new teachers: Does this kind of church development depend on a conservative theological vision? Or could people with mainstream theology also generate a thriving, entrepreneurial, ecclesiastical system? My answer to these questions, which I presented in an essay published in *Encounter*, was that churches holding a theological center quite different from that of Perimeter Church could also generate large congregations.[41] I discussed four characteristics I believed would need to be in place. Effective churches, regardless of denomination and theological position, would be vision-driven, culturally relevant, and able to distribute responsibility for pastoral care to many members of the congregation. Leaders at the Perimeter seminar told us that the music in worship was highly important. Although the examples we saw at Perimeter Church itself were contemporary gospel, we were told that in some cultural settings the music would be drawn primarily from standard mainline sources. The music would be determined by the cultural styles and standards in the community where a church was to be established.

The impact of these new teachers was a recovery of excitement in my teaching. It was as though a defibrillator had been applied to reestablish rhythm to my understanding of pastoral work. I was persuaded once again that mainline churches could gain new spiritual energy and institutional strength. I tried to instill this sense of hope in students by introducing them to this literature and

---

[41] I phrased this question in slightly different wording in an article describing the Perimeter Church: Keith Watkins, "Vision-Driven Ministry: Reflections on Atlanta's Perimeter Church and Perimeter Ministries International," *Encounter* 56, no. 3 (Summer 1995), 289–309.

encouraging those with positive experiences of church renewal to share their stories. Some of my students seemed to be heartened by these classes. Others, however, indicated that, while this kind of renewal might be possible in some congregations, they were stuck with old-style churches with no chance of transformation.

Two books published during the early 1990s helped me conclude this period of thinking about congregational vitality. Although the authors represented two sharply contrasting ecclesial traditions, both dealt with the relationship between worship and evangelism. Both were highly critical of the current practices in the churches to whom they addressed their books. Both presented an interpretation of the problems in their ecclesial communities and recommended a new way for pastors, musicians, and other church leaders to develop their ministries. Despite significant differences between these two writers, there was an amazing correspondence of views concerning these matters.

Patrick R. Keifert, a Lutheran professor of theology, titled his book, *Welcoming the Stranger: A Public Theology of Worship and Evangelism*.[42] Countering the assumption that worship and evangelism do not belong together, he intended to show "that liturgical worship and effective evangelism can complement and enhance one another." By liturgical worship he meant the historic public liturgy of the church in which the people in the congregation were active participants rather than passive observers. He understood evangelism to be "proclaiming the good news and leading people to a public identity in Christ."[43] Rather than opposing one another, Keifert insisted, "liturgical worship and evangelism belong together in a mutual apostolic mission." His diagnosis was that in recent times worship had moved from being a public act of the church to one that was shaped by expectations that belong primarily to the private spheres of life. Pastors and people alike were using individualism and intimacy as the criteria for determining the characteristics of worship and, as a result, were making it increasingly difficult for strangers—the outsiders—to find their way into churches. He discussed three liturgical reform movements during the past century: the nineteenth-century aesthetic movement, symbolized by

---

[42] Patrick R. Keifert, *Welcoming the Stranger: A Public Theology of Worship and Evangelism* (Minneapolis: Fortress, 1992).
[43] Ibid., 5.

the Gothic church architecture; the mid-twentieth-century renewal based on biblical theology and patristic liturgical convictions; and the celebrationist movement in the 1960s and 1970s. Although Keifert approved many aspects of these movements, he faulted all of them for intensifying the process by which worship lost its public character and became part of the private life of churches.

Keifert believed, however, that a modified liturgical worship, culturally adapted to our time, would be the most effective evangelistic agent that churches could use. One of the reasons was that public ritual represents feelings and values—and here I heard echoes of Susanne K. Langer—that worshipers could observe and claim to whatever degree they found themselves ready to claim. Keifert contrasted this presentational character of worship with a parallel idea—that worship expresses emotion directly. When worshipers encounter feelings and values in so direct a mode, they draw back and are inhibited from participating. He showed how participation in ritual enables people to move from their isolation into communion with God and with other worshipers because it allows them to do so without forcing them to expose their inner feelings to other people. In this kind of public act, people can begin the process of reordering their lives. Keifert believed, however, that liturgical worship needed to be more attentive to contemporary experience in order for its evangelistic potential to be realized, and he offered a four-step planning process for church leaders to follow. The purpose of the planning, done by experienced leaders, was "to plan, practice, and reflect on worship so that God's liberative presence is disclosed in worship and the people of God are drawn into and receive this presence with prayer, praise, and thanksgiving."[44]

Sally Morgenthaler was trained in music education and worked as a worship coordinator. Although she referred to the influence of a Lutheran church on her experience and understanding, her primary references were to megachurches in the evangelical movement. The center of gravity for her book was suggested in its title: *Worship Evangelism: Inviting Unbelievers into the Presence of God*.[45] Morgenthaler was convinced that, despite their apparent success, the evangelical megachurches were in trouble. Many of

---

[44] Ibid., 147.
[45] Sally Morgenthaler, *Worship Evangelism: Inviting Unbelievers into the Presence of God* (Grand Rapids, MI: Zondervan, 1995).

their members had come from other churches, and the percentage of the American adult population that attended church continued to decline. Furthermore, she believed, many of the people who participated in these churches dropped out a little later on. The slick and entertaining productions on Sundays were failing to give the attenders what they were hoping for—a sense of direct experience with God. The core of her argument was that these churches no longer worshiped God, and therefore denied participants the opportunity of coming into the immediate presence of God. Morgenthaler showed how the very audiences the megachurches targeted—the young unchurched—were likely not to be reached in significant numbers by these counterfeit worship events. Even Boomers, Busters, and other young generations were not long interested in events that had lost their focus on God and had become self-help activities.

Although Morgenthaler lacked Keifert's interest in liturgical worship, she did recommend that worship leaders seek to repackage tradition, using cultural forms from contemporary life as the packaging materials. Some of the music used in these churches, for example, could be drawn from the traditional body of church music but be played and sung in new ways. Morgenthaler believed that participation in genuine worship was more effective as an evangelistic method than being a passive observer in a seeker service. Thus, she argued for "open worship," in which seekers and believers would be present side by side. Seekers did not need to participate but would, in all likelihood, find themselves drawn into the pattern of words and actions of active worshipers. She was especially urgent in her discussion of music as a key element in services that sought to be helpful both to believers and seekers.

In contrast to Keifert, Morgenthaler had no ties with the historic liturgies of the word and table. Instead, she functioned with "five action categories" or verbs: esteem or glorify God, expound the gospel, encounter the God who inhabits our praise, examine our lives as a result of encountering God, and enjoy God's benefits and love.[46] Although the elements were different, the sequence reminded me of the one used by G. Edwin Osborn forty-five years earlier in the order of worship he had recommended for Disciples worship: an act of reverence, an act of fellowship, an act of dedication, and an

---

[46] Ibid., 159–160.

act of renewal.[47] Despite the difference in tone, these two lists are efforts to develop a liturgical sequence that fosters the immediate sense of God's presence during the words and actions of the service. Morgenthaler believed the various elements that churches use in their worship services could be arranged in many different sequences, so long as they developed the five action categories in the order that she specified. She distinguished between energy and intensity, suggesting that for younger people services needed to begin with music and actions of high energy; only then could congregants develop the vulnerability by which they could open themselves to God. During this middle period, the energy level would subside, but the intensity level would increase. The service would close with more high-energy elements as the transition back into ordinary life.

One of the churches she offered as an illustration was St. Timothy's Catholic Church in Mesa, Arizona, where the teen mass each Sunday evening regularly was attended by 1,400 people, most of them in their teens and twenties. I had already heard about this service from Disciples friends and attended to experience it for myself. The event was designed for teens, and much of the leadership was provided by people of that age. They did the full order of the mass, with three scripture readings, a psalm, sermon, prayers, offering, the eucharistic prayer, and communion in both kinds presented to the entire congregation. Yet the music and the style of celebration communicated directly with the culture of the intended congregation. It was a remarkably clear example of "repackaged tradition," to use Morgenthaler's phrase.[48] The sermon was an impassioned presentation of the need for people to encounter Christ and be transformed through that encounter. It seemed more evangelical than Catholic. The pastor invited teens to come around the altar during the intercessions following the sermon and he prayed, again in an impassioned way, for them to encounter Christ.

My evenings at St. Timothy's Church confirmed my conviction that the classic liturgy of word and table, done with culturally directed music and expressing a strong message of new life through Jesus Christ, can be a strong contender for the hearts and lives of

---

[47] G. Edwin Osborn, *Christian Worship: A Service Book* (St. Louis: Christian Board of Publication, 1953), 3–4.

[48] Sally Morgenthaler, *Worship Evangelism*, 136.

people in contemporary American culture. In general, however, the only churches I found that exhibited this capacity were Roman Catholic. Morgenthaler reported that 40 percent of Baby Busters described the Catholic Church as their "spiritual home." Although many church growth experts were puzzled by this fact, Morgenthaler's explanation was that this generation "with the *least* sense of rootedness and stability … is looking for experiences and institutions that have some permanence about them."[49]

As I moved past sixty years of age, I realized that I had read too many books and student papers, attended too many faculty meetings, and spent too much time thinking about the challenges of eucharistic worship, Christian unity, and the vitality of congregation life. My new teachers in the books I was reading were energizing my spirit and elevating my sense of hope. They were confirming in a surprising way the insight about worship that had guided my work all through the years—that it combine catholic substance and protestant spirit. I was coming to a more flexible understanding of the catholic core of the church's liturgical life and a more dynamic and culturally aware understanding of the spirit that needed to operate. Although I was not thinking about the "churches of the third type" that I had described in *Liturgies in a Time When Cities Burn*, that was what I was still hoping to see come into prominence.

I decided it was time to return to the pastorate, where I could devote my major attention to developing these qualities in a mainline congregation. It was in this mood that I gladly retired from my career as seminary professor and started a new post-career challenge—to be founding pastor of a new congregation that would be catholic in substance and protestant in spirit.

Mesa de Cristo Christian Church

My interest in new church establishment was stimulated by Dean Joe R. Jones, when he asked that I develop a course on evangelism for mainline churches. He agreed that a seminar on establishing new mainstream congregations offered by Pacific School of Religion would be good preparation for part of the new course. The teacher was a United Methodist pastor from Phoenix who had just completed a term on the conference staff in which more than twenty new Methodist congregations had been established in

---

[49] Ibid., 131.

Arizona during a five-year period. His seminar demonstrated that mainline churches could be successful in new church development and that the best way to begin was with a pastor who called a congregation into being and then began the task of looking for land and constructing its own building. Although he had been insistent that his new congregations would be Methodist and mainline, he was ready to adopt methodologies from evangelical churches. I became convinced that this low-cost approach was the right way to create new congregations. I also was encouraged to believe that unchurched people could be attracted to congregations that proclaimed the Christian faith and life in ways that were common in mainline congregations.

During this same period near the conclusion of my seminary career, I consulted with Deborah Thompson, who headed the new church program for Disciples, and attended training programs that she directed. At one of these events, I met Benny and Elaine Boling, only a few years younger than myself, who were beginning a new congregation on the edge of Springfield, Missouri. They had also been reading in the literature of new church development that emphasized vision-based ministry, low-cost beginnings, a gift-centered approach to the ministries of church members, and an appeal to unchurched people. Their new congregation—Gateway Christian Church—was in its early stages of development using this model.

About a year before my retirement, I had the opportunity of working in a new church start-up based on the very ideas I believed could be effective among Disciples. A group of Disciples congregations in Hamilton County, one of the fastest growing sections of the metropolitan Indianapolis area, agreed to sponsor a new church in the town of Fishers, which was beginning to develop as a new edge city. The organizing pastor was Terri Gomez, a graduate of Brite Divinity School and pastor in a small community in Missouri. When we talked in my office at the seminary, I was encouraged because she too wanted to start a church that would clothe a full liturgy of word and sacrament in a musical and cultural form that would be appealing to unchurched, younger adults. Gomez was committed to the idea that the church would surround this new kind of celebration with cells, small groups in which people would learn to read and understand the Bible, support one another as they grew in the Christian faith, and engage in mission. I volunteered to be part of the group she was drawing together to form this new congregation.

We spent the early months with Sunday evening meetings for Bible study, prayer, and conversation about the church we hoped to establish. We found a temporary location for worship and education and developed plans for using a telephoning program to develop a large list of people who would be interested in receiving mailings about the new church. During this direct mail campaign, we began meeting on Sunday mornings so that we could "practice" our worship service and be sure that everything was ready for the new people who would come to the grand opening service. Although we had followed the start-up manual closely, our responses were on the low end of the averages the manual had forecast. Even so, our first Sunday was an exciting and satisfying time for all of us who had worked hard in preparation, and we moved forward in the next few weeks to solidify a group who would become the core for the new church. I found Gomez's preaching to be interesting and inviting, and her liturgical sense to be strong. Our Sunday morning service was similar in content to those I often planned at the seminary, although the music and style were more popular. I was satisfied that we were presenting a way of worship that could appeal to people with little church background and to others who had been in church much of their lives.

Two Bible study groups were formed, but we found that they did not generate new groups as we had hoped. Our temporary quarters, although marginally adequate, needed to be upgraded. We were able to lease space in a small business mall, and with much effort on the part of congregants, we remodeled it into a center for worship and meetings and an office for our pastor. Despite our hard work, the congregation grew more slowly than we had expected. Although we were gaining new participants as quickly as many conventional church starts did, our model had encouraged us to anticipate much more rapid growth. Our failure to multiply discouraged many of the participants, created too much work for others of the group, and left us vulnerable to mounting financial pressure. Support from the churches that had sponsored the idea of a new church had never been strong, and the new church program of Indiana Disciples had not embraced the project. When I moved from Indianapolis to Arizona, the new congregation seemed viable although fragile.

The Gateway start-up in Springfield, Missouri, seemed sturdier. The organizing pastor was a mature leader who had previously served large, flourishing congregations. He was called to Springfield by a group of six Disciples congregations in the city. It was made clear to him, however, that he was not to take members away from those congregations or ask them for financial help beyond the program budget that had been established for the new church. This low-cost startup was in sharp contrast to that of an Assemblies of God congregation that started at the same time with a membership of 900 provided by other Assemblies congregations and a line of credit of six million dollars. Benny and Elaine Boling seemed to me to be doing everything right. They started with about sixty congregants, but this congregation also grew slowly. In seven years, average attendance more than doubled what it had been in its first months. Meantime, the Assemblies congregation grew fourfold.

Despite the disappointing results at Fishers and Gateway, I was persuaded by the success of Arizona Methodists that the effort to create a church that was catholic in substance and protestant in spirit could work in Arizona. The new church development committee was agreeable to the approach I recommended and offered financial support and limited assistance by volunteers from other Disciples congregations in the area. It was understood from the beginning that we would, like the United Methodist Church in Arizona, work on developing a congregation before we tried to find land, create a building fund, and construct a building.

My first objective was to understand the community that had been chosen for the new church. The Arizona new church committee had decided that the Northwest Valley on the edge of Phoenix—the Sun Cities community—would be the site. For several months before moving to Arizona, I read a weekly newspaper published in Sun City West, where we had decided to establish our home. My goal was to learn about the social dynamics of the mission field where we would work, including the pressure points that could become the focus for mission. A short history of Sun City, in a book by John M. Findlay, provided the historical and cultural context and alerted me to the long-standing resistance of people in the retirement communities to pay taxes for public schools.[50] The new church committee bought

---

[50] John M. Findlay, "Sun City, Arizona: New Town for Old Folks." In John M. Findlay, *Magic Lands: Western Cityscapes and American Culture After 1940* (Berkeley, CA: University of California Press, 1992).

demographic projections for this section of metropolitan Phoenix, and I studied them carefully. After moving to Arizona, I confirmed these studies by conversations with people in leadership positions in the city of Surprise, the Dysart public schools, and the Del Webb Corporation. I also talked extensively with members of a support team from nearby Disciples congregations and with the new church development committee.

I was persuaded by the projections that the city of Surprise would grow rapidly and that much of this growth would consist of families and working people for whom there currently was no church. To my surprise and growing frustration, strong voices in the Sun City and Sun City West communities scoffed at these projections and questioned the possibility of creating churches for a family population. The mindset of some in Sun City West was expressed when they objected to a proposed family development near Sun City West: It would put pressure on our churches. We would have to deal with children and build a Sunday school.

In contrast to this point of view, I was convinced that it was time to create a congregation that would embrace this general population in addition to the retired people who were the exclusive constituency of the existing Sun Cities area churches. The plan that emerged was that we would undertake a two-stage development. Because the retirement community was already present and continuing to grow rapidly, we would focus on this population in the first phase of our work—from December through the spring and summer of our first year. Assuming that we could stabilize a congregation consisting primarily of retired people, we would then move in our second year to begin a second worship service that would be designed to appeal to a much younger constituency, including children. My hope was that the financial support from the senior congregation would make possible the expansion of our ministry as the younger portion of Surprise and surrounding communities began to grow.

From the beginning, I was determined that our worship would be consistent with the principles that had shaped my work through the years. It would be a full service of word and sacrament, conducted in an open style that would be accessible to people with little or no previous experience in churches but at the same time reasonably familiar to people who had been longtime churchgoers. Initially, we referred to the project as Northwest Valley Christian Church, but advisors recommended that a name more descriptive of the new congregation's character be chosen before we launched the church. I developed a list that ranged from traditional titles like Christ Church to others that were widely used in new church startups such as New Hope Church.

Then I remembered a precedent-setting church that had been formed in New York City during the mid-nineteenth century—The Church of the Holy Communion. Here, worship was designed to bring the Eucharist to ordinary people and to develop a strong ministry of social service to several distressed populations of the city. I was attracted to the word *mesa*, Spanish for table, which is much used in the Southwest, as in names like Mesa Verde. Several streams of thought seemed to come together in the name Mesa de Cristo Christian Church. I assumed that most people would quickly abbreviate to Mesa de Cristo Church, or to the even shorter Mesa de Cristo. After trying out the idea with several advisors, I recommended that this be the name for the new congregation. As a logo, I adapted a design from Rudolf Schwarz's book, *The Church Incarnate: The Sacred Function of Christian Architecture*, a box-shaped table on a slight platform, topped by a half circle that hovers over it like a dome.[51] I developed a motto to go with the church's name: "Gathered at Christ's Table, Where All Are Fed." The combination, it seemed to me, stated what kind of a church we would be. It was Southwestern in ethos. It transcended denominational identity while expressing our Disciples' heritage. What I didn't anticipate then but discern now is that it also anticipated the change that since then has taken place, from seeing this action as the means of uniting separated denominations to proclaiming that gathering at this table is a way of bringing wholeness to a fragmented human community.

I knew that music would be a key to our service, but I didn't know how to find musicians who could provide the entrée into strong, contemporary, liturgical song. A young executive with the Del Webb Corporation told me about the Sunday Masses at the Franciscan Renewal Center north of Scottsdale, and I saw its approach to worship as a model for our own. I had no success in finding musicians who could lead our venture in a similar style. The music team with which we began, however, was quite interesting and worked out

---

[51] Rudolf Schwarz, *The Church Incarnate: The Sacred Function of Church Architecture* (Chicago: Henry Regnery, 1958), 35–38.

rather well. A traditional church musician, with strong Disciples heritage, now retired in Sun City West, became our keyboard person, and a young woman—a Baptist college student and experienced club singer—became the one to lead congregational song and sing a solo each week. The hymns and choruses in the newly published *Chalice Hymnal* provided a good range of music for our initial period, and I decided to use that resource even though we would not initially put hymnals in the hands of worshipers. We included a psalm in each service, even though the manner of singing psalms in worship was new to the musicians and most of the congregants.

I wanted to continue certain Disciples practices, especially lay leadership at the communion table, but at the same time to build in measures that would replace some of the shortcomings of most Disciples liturgies. As the pastor, I offered the prayer at the communion table, developing a new text each week. These prayers were focused on remembering Jesus and his self-giving for the sake of the world, but they were brief and contemporary in language. The invitation to the table was adapted from one that was used at All Saints Episcopal Church in Pasadena, California: "Whoever you are, wherever you are in your journey of faith, you are welcome at this table."

In order to develop an initial constituency, we did cold telephoning to develop a list of people for a direct-mail campaign. As in Fishers, however, the results were at the low end of the scale, even though this phase of our work was directed by a person with extensive experience in this approach to building a constituency. We started on the first Sunday of Advent with a service attended by some 200 people, including friends from the Sun City Christian Church and other congregations in the area. I followed up with calls on many of the people and further mailings. We quickly settled into a pattern with about fifty people in attendance, most of them from the retirement communities that dominated our part of the valley. By Easter, it had become clear that growth was not coming as we had expected and that we would not be able to start a second service in the fall. One of the people who joined us during that first season had a strong background in Christian education, and she agreed to work at developing a program that could be attractive to children so that we would have a better chance of appealing to younger families. The blended style of music seemed to suit the mixed congregation.

Some people responded positively to my preaching, but others were like one of our younger members, who confessed to me after service one Sunday that she was bored sick by my sermons.

During the summer, a Baptist church that was meeting at nearby Kingswood School closed, and we were able to use a meeting room in that building. We bought chairs and other minimal equipment and started in the fall with a new wave of hope. This change of location moved us into the geographical heart of the Surprise-Dysart community. It was a harbinger of hope for me when on the first Sunday in the school we were joined in worship by a family of three who represented the old ranching and cultural leadership of the Northwest Valley. Soon thereafter the mayor of Surprise became a frequent participant in worship. A few other new families joined our effort, and there was reason to believe that we would move forward, although at a slower rate than we had hoped. Other families with children would come once and not return. Clearly, our style of service and church was not what they were looking for.

Even before we had begun holding services, however, I had begun to develop feelings of panic about this venture. During the first spring that the congregation was meeting, I met regularly with a counselor, who diagnosed my condition as clinical depression. Although he recommended that I begin taking an antidepressant, I refused, trying to follow his guidance on revising my work pattern and developing a new way of thinking about our venture. During the summer, I felt better, but as fall approached the depression returned. I went back to the counselor knowing that there would be no choice but to begin taking the medication he recommended. During the program year, attendance grew slightly but stress developed within the critical core of the congregation. My assessment as we came to the second Easter was that the loss of strength at the core outweighed the gains we were making in the wider circle of our membership. Unwilling to continue with the medication, I consulted with the new church committee in Arizona and staff of the Disciples new church program, and then retired from my work with the congregation. An ad interim minister was selected and the work continued, although with a new name and a significant shift in its direction, becoming a more conventional mainstream kind of church. After another year, the congregation discontinued its ministry.

Despite the closing of Mesa de Cristo Christian Church, the merit of attempting to build a cross-generational church has been confirmed by later developments. Between 1995 and 2000, a dozen congregations were established in the Sun City West–Surprise–Dysart area, and all but two or three intended to build in the multigenerational community rather than in an age-restricted area. The congregation established in Sun City Grand by the Evangelical Lutheran Church of America has achieved significant growth, as have three evangelical churches and a Catholic church established in the multigenerational portion of Surprise and the unincorporated areas just south of the city. The United Methodist and Presbyterian Churches and the United Church of Christ have chosen to establish churches for the entire life cycle rather than to continue their previous Sun Cities pattern of building churches for an age-restricted population.

Even though I had tried to understand the social dynamics of the Northwest Valley, I had not realized how great the tension was between the retirement communities and the family-oriented communities. Ever since the first Sun City was established in 1961, the flash point had been paying taxes for the support of public schools. During the early months of my work with Mesa de Cristo, this conflict developed again, instigated by people living near us in Sun City West, and I found my sympathies increasingly moving toward the Surprise–Dysart position and away from the Sun City West position. I could see more clearly than at the beginning that the contrast between retirement and family-oriented congregations is so great that a church start-up had to focus on one or the other. If the initial emphasis was to create a church consisting primarily of seniors, it would have been nearly impossible to take the next step and create a church for younger adults, teens, and children. If a multigenerational church was established, with a focus on younger people, many older people might also come.

My efforts to reach out to the leadership of the larger community, especially in the schools and city government, helped us attract a diversified constituency and connected us with people who were committed to community leadership. I found it more difficult, however, to develop a readiness to engage in mission among the people of the congregation. Nor could I develop a viable educational dimension to the congregation's life. We were, however, attracting families with a growing number of children. If I had been able to stay with Mesa de Cristo Church, we could probably have become a viable congregation. It is not difficult to project a moderate rate of growth—perhaps 10 percent per year—which would have brought us to an attendance after five years of eighty to one hundred per Sunday during the main seasons of the year.

During the two years I worked on this project, I discovered that I am not very good in overcoming conflict among leaders and in maintaining a strong sense of coherent leadership in the venture. I can think things through better than I can carry things out. In the final conversation with my counselor, he noted that perhaps it was not an accident that I had spent most of my career as a professor rather than as a pastor.

The important question, however, has to do with the religious life of the congregation we were attempting. Were the liturgical form and message appropriate for establishing a new church for unchurched, younger people? I followed the lectionary in my preaching and tried to orient my messages toward the new life that God offers in Jesus Christ. References to how we ought to live were subsidiary to this main message. I later noticed in large newspaper ads that evangelical start-ups reversed that emphasis. Their sermons seemed to be problem-solving, starting with problems in family life and work, and then moving toward a resolution that comes from God. In the years following the closing of Mesa de Cristo, three evangelical churches that had started in the Surprise community experienced dramatic growth, one of them increasing more rapidly than any other Assemblies of God church in the nation. In their book *Rerouting the Protestant Mainstream*, C. Kirk Hadaway and David A. Roozen suggest that churches that I am calling evangelical employ much that is secular and remove much of what is ordinarily considered sacred. This "seemingly secular public face," however masks "a strong evangelical ethos." They are using secular honey to get people into the hive; once they are in the hive, they are drawn into the deeply religious aspects of the congregation and into the alternative world of personal and social relationships that the congregation has developed.[52]

---

[52] C. Kirk Hadaway and David A. Roozen, *Rerouting the Protestant Mainstream: Sources of Growth and Opportunities for Change* (Nashville, TN: Abingdon Press, 1995), 50.

At Mesa de Cristo, the service was explicitly religious, which meant that people had to respond favorably from their first encounter with us. Some who came to our new church were not involved in church life or religious practice, but they found a message in our services that God offers a different and better way of life. One person mentioned in a discussion group that he and his wife both had had "eventful lives." They came to our church in the hope that the gospel would help them discover the new life that Jesus promises. They were baptized, fully expecting that the new life would begin. We were unable, however, to provide the nurture and support they needed to be transformed in attitudes, habits, and practices. The result was that they quickly became disillusioned and experienced even greater disorganization in life than before. The experience of these two people was indicative of what seemed to be happening to others. Finding the message believable and the environment inviting, they ventured forth only to be disappointed at the next phase of their experience in the congregation.

During these years, some churches that emphasized a religious message and eucharistic worship did come into being in the Northwest Valley section of metropolitan Phoenix and experience rapid growth, but they were mostly Roman Catholic. The founding priest of one of these Catholic communities spoke of building a church on worship (the regular celebration of the Mass), education, and community service. These churches based on the eucharistic liturgy of word and table appealed to the general public—young and old, popular and classical in their aesthetics, experienced in church-going and new to the Christian faith. More than Protestant churches I knew, these new Catholic churches embodied the characteristics of what I have called churches of the third type.

The deepening puzzle, as I moved deeper into retirement, was why Catholic churches more than Protestant congregations seemed able to embody these characteristics and thrive.

Five

Historian at Work and Play

When I completed my work with Mesa de Cristo Christian Church, I was, for the first time, fully retired. No classes or sermons to prepare, no books that had to be read, no church-related meetings I had to attend. One continuing activity was participation in the Surprise–Grand-Bell Rotary Club I had joined soon after moving to Sun City West. Although I had little previous experience with service clubs, I joined one as a way of getting acquainted with the community and participating constructively toward its well-being. The members of our club, which met weekly for breakfast, included people from Sun City West and Surprise who were active in their business and professional lives and a similar number of retired people. Perhaps a third of the membership lived in Arizona only during the winter months. Two people I met in these meetings became charter members of the Mesa de Cristo church.

A year after my pastoral activities closed, I was elected president of the club, which increased the attention I gave to the workings of Rotary International. As president of a local club, I was expected to attend the annual district conventions, and I participated in two of these gatherings of men and women from all across northern Arizona, one in Prescott, a city in Arizona's high country about ninety-five miles from my home in the Valley of the Sun, and the other in Parker on the Colorado River, about 140 miles from home. I traveled to both cities by bicycle, which gave me a more direct sense of Arizona's "outback" and the people who live there. One aspect of Rotary that impressed me was its approach to service projects, especially those outside of the United States. A club in the United States would select a project, such as establishing a well to provide fresh water for a community in India, and raise needed funds. A delegation from the club then traveled to the location and, in partnership with a Rotary club in the region being served, would do the work they had planned. This pattern of partnership seemed like an ideal way for churches to participate in overseas missionary projects.

One of the satisfying aspects of full retirement was that I could extend the range of my bicycling. Sun City West was then on the western edge of metropolitan Phoenix, and a wide swath of land west and north of our home was open desert with only scattered villages. One was named Nadaburg, from the Spanish word that means nothing, and this name seemed right for much of the territory I explored on two wheels. In addition to riding up Grand Avenue thirty-three miles to Wickenburg for coffee at the McDonald's and back, there was another long ride, thirty-five miles west and south on Bell Road/Sun Valley Parkway around two sides of the White Tank Mountains and back. Other routes of varying lengths took me over all kinds of secondary roads in land still vacant but soon to be developed. In the 1990s, the Sun Valley Parkway, with the White Tank Mountains on one side and open desert on the other, had little traffic other than coyotes, roadrunners, and cyclists. One Fourth of July I was cycling alone through an isolated stretch of the desert and came across a human corpse on the side of the highway. With ample amounts of sunscreen and water, I became a serious, solo cyclist in the hot desert sun.

One of the books that I read during this period was Jim Fixx's *Complete Book of Running*, and on one of my rides something from that book triggered a new way of understanding myself. When it came to cycling, I was an *athlete*. I rode in a disciplined manner, giving careful attention to diet and technique. I rode on a regular basis and tried to maintain good form. Although I competed only against myself and occasionally for short distances with other guys I met on the road, I was nevertheless an athlete.

During these regular rides, most of them solo, I became increasingly interested in the environmental, historical, and cultural features of the territories through which my two-wheeled travels carried me. I was fascinated by the rivers, which in most of Arizona, New Mexico, and Southern California are part of the Colorado River system, and by the relationships between the rivers and aquifers. Equally interesting was the relationship between the limited water supplies and the civilizations that had come and gone in generations past. I was fascinated, and increasingly apprehensive, because of the contradictions of rapidly increasing urbanization in arid lands and rapidly diminishing water sources. Following my return to the well-watered Pacific Northwest, and more recently to the well-watered Midwest, the relations of water and civilization have continued to occupy much of my time. Just as I had realized that my activities had made me an athlete, I was developing an additional, perhaps more serious interest. I now could see that I was also becoming an *environmentalist.*

Free to Do My Real Work

Early in my tenure as seminary professor, while reading a book on gerontology, I encountered an idea that has stayed with me ever since: Retirement allows people to continue their *work* without the constraints of a *job*. Although I was enjoying my life as a Rotarian and bicyclist, I was becoming restless and soon realized that it was time to get on with my work. So, what was my work? The answer to that question, I soon realized, had been implied by the pastoral counselor with whom I had consulted during my attempt to start a new church. He encouraged me to spend one morning each week at the library of Arizona State West, the university's branch in Glendale, close to our Sun City West home. Immediately, I had felt at home because of other people nearby intent on learning, coffee close at hand, and with the freedom to read and write in response to intellectual urgings. I enjoyed my trips to the library and continued the habit even when the original reason for going no longer was a factor.

Now that I was fully retired, I could focus my reading and writing on Christian worship, and on other historically oriented scholarly work. My scholarly identity was confirmed by the invitation to become a member of the Association for Theological Discussion (ATD) sponsored by the Disciples Seminary Foundation in Claremont, California. It had been created many years earlier by Ronald Osborn, who had moved from CTS to teach church history at the School of Theology in Claremont, and Donald Reisinger, president of the Disciples Seminary Foundation. Their purpose had been to bring professors and pastors together, so that pastors would think more theologically and professors would think more pastorally. By the time I joined, the energies of the ATD had diminished. Only two or three professors participated and some of the pastors were retired from their ministries. Even so, the annual drives across Arizona to Southern California with a friend, who taught religious studies at Arizona State's main campus in Tempe, were enjoyable, and the focused conversations on pastoral theology in the ATD meetings were challenging.

Early in my Arizona years I came across the books of Gary Paul Nabhan that opened a new intellectual world to me. He was born into an Arab-American family in Gary, Indiana, and came to Tucson for college and graduate studies at the University of Arizona. He was appointed to the university faculty, specializing in research and writing on the natural history of desert plants and animals as it relates to a dying agricultural tradition. He gave special attention to the cultural history of the Tohono O'odham people. I have never met him or heard him lecture, and I have had only casual relationships with Native peoples in these desert lands. Even so, Nabhan's work continues to enrich my sense of Indigenous cultures in Western sections of the United States. I have wondered how this body of knowledge might have affected my work if I had become acquainted with it during my years on the faculty of CTS.

On alternate Sundays, I attended Sun City Christian Church, where a former student of mine at CTS was pastor, and Foothills Christian Church, where the co-pastors were a married couple I had known since they were in high school and befriended when they were students at Pacific School of Religion. Often, I attended an early Mass at Prince of Peace Catholic Church in Sun City West, and occasionally I attended other churches that interested me, such as the Community Church of Joy, a mega-church near us that retained its identification with the Lutheran Church in America even though its liturgical life seemed not very Lutheran. I continued my interest in the youth Mass at St. Timothy's Catholic Church in Mesa, on the other side of metropolitan Phoenix. Friends had called this congregation to my attention, and it was described as an example of good churchly practice by Sally Morgenthaler in her 1995 book *Worship Evangelism: Inviting Unbelievers into the Presence of God*. I also read literature about the church growth movement, developed by Don McGavran, formerly a Disciples missionary in India and lecturer at the School of Religion when I was a student. His dreams of creating an American version of people-based evangelism that he had developed in India did not find a permanent home in a Disciples' institution, but flourished at Fuller Theological Seminary in Pasadena, California.

The one part of my work that was clearly focused and disciplined during this period was writing a history of Christian Theological Seminary. While still teaching, I had written a forty-page paper giving a summary of the history as I had experienced it, beginning with accounts I had heard from some of my college professors and their friends who had studied at Butler before I had begun my studies. President Richard Dickinson asked permission to distribute the paper to the faculty and trustees. He then proposed that I write a full history of the seminary and its previous connections with Butler University. Trips to Claremont and Indianapolis gave me access to periodicals, especially *Encounter* and its predecessor, *The Shane Quarterly*, and to the large stores of archival material at CTS. Although much of what I had written over the years had been historically oriented, work on this book was the first piece of sustained and serious historical research since my doctoral dissertation on New England Puritanism ecclesiology, which I had researched and written during my first three years as professor of practical theology at CTS.[1]

At this point, I knew what my schedule would be: During the long, hot, Arizona summers, cycling came early in the mornings and scholarly activities in afternoons. A weather-related alternating pattern of reading, writing, and riding has continued ever since. Whereas some road cyclists look for brew pubs on their long rides, my tendency is to look for bookstores and museums. I have found them in interesting, often remote places, Cathlamet, Washington; Bisbee and Patagonia, Arizona; Alpine, Texas; and Fernandina Beach, Florida, among them. My multi-day bike trips have been shaped, in part, by my interest in exploring historical scenes and in experiencing for myself the environmental issues that anchor my historical and environmental interests. My theological focus, however, has continued to be the church's life at the Lord's table as the source of our unity in Jesus Christ.

---

[1] Keith Watkins, *The Ecclesiastical Contributions of Increase Mather to Late Seventeenth and Early Eighteenth Century Puritan Thought.* Doctoral dissertation, Pacific School of Religion, Berkeley, California, 1964.

Continuing Work in the Christian Unity Movement

On a sunny Sunday afternoon in 1999, I attended a special celebration at Desert Palms Presbyterian Church on Star Dust Boulevard in Sun City West. Participating were leaders of four Protestant churches: the Evangelical Lutheran Church in America, the Presbyterian Church (USA), the Reformed Church in America, and the United Church of Christ. Their purpose was to activate "A Formula of Agreement for the Orderly Exchange of Ordained Ministers of Word and Table" that the denominations had established in 1997. In its preface, the "Formula" states that the "timing reflects a doctrinal consensus which has been developing over the past thirty-two years coupled with an increasing urgency for the church to proclaim a gospel of unity in contemporary society." The purpose of this agreement was for these four churches to enter into "full communion," by which they agreed that each one recognized the others as churches. They would "recognize each other's Baptism and authorize and encourage the sharing of the Lord's supper among their members; recognize each other's various ministries and make provision for the orderly exchange of ordained ministers of Word and Sacrament"; and they would commit themselves to orderly processes of consultation, decision making, theological dialogue, and public witness. They would "pledge themselves to living together under the Gospel in such a way that the principle of mutual affirmation and admonition becomes the basis of a trusting relationship in which respect and love for the other will have a chance to grow."

I rejoiced that these churches were moving together in this strong, public way. Although their agreement was more modest in scope than agreements proposed by the Consultation on Church Union, these "four churches of Reformation heritage" were manifesting a similar spirit and accomplishing several of COCU's objectives. A basis for living together in faith, worship, and mission while continuing in separate ecclesial households was being established.

I was puzzled and disappointed that my own church was not a partner in the new relationship defined in "A Formula of Agreement." Had the Disciples Council on Christian Unity chosen not to participate in the long period of consultation that had taken place? Were we not understood—within our own ranks or by other churches—to be Reformed? Were we not a church "of Reformation heritage?"

Underneath these questions, a more disquieting fear darkened my efforts to understand why we were not part of the proceedings on this sunny afternoon. I had first expressed these ideas in the thesis I had written as a seminarian at the Butler School of Religion. I agreed with two Disciples leaders of that period, Virgil Sly and Ronald Osborn, both of whom believed that if Disciples continued the way they were, they would find themselves "remaining in the status of a small, aloof sect in a world where denominations are drawing together."[2] Offsetting this uneasiness was the fact that the Consultation on Church Union was still in the background. The possibility still remained that the participating churches, including the Disciples, would establish A Church of Christ Uniting and keep my church in the Protestant mainstream.

In January 1998, less than a year after the Sun City West event, the Consultation met for its eighteenth plenary assembly under the leadership of President Vivian U. Robinson and Interim General Secretary Lewis H. Lancaster Jr. It was clear that the churches were not ready to go forward to create the new church they had envisioned. The question they faced was this: How could COCU's vision be redefined "to attract the ecumenical energy of the churches?" Disciples scholar and ecumenist Michael K. Kinnamon chaired the committee that drafted a proposed course of action. The delegates voted to terminate the Consultation on Church Union and create a new relationship entitled Churches Uniting in Christ to continue the search for greater unity. Their hope was that the nine COCU churches would continue and that others, especially the Evangelical Lutheran Church in America, would take a more active role in the process. They projected a date, three years later, when this transformation would take place and elected Kinnamon to be COCU's part-time general secretary during this final term of the Consultation's life.

The heart of the proposal was a list of nine "visible marks of Churches Uniting in Christ." The first four marks were the classic theological factors that Eugene Carson Blake had identified in his sermon thirty-eight years earlier and that had been central to COCU's work ever since: (1) mutual recognition of one another as authentic expressions of the one Church of Jesus Christ, (2) mutual

---

[2] Ronald E. Osborn, "Problems of Disciple Participating in the Ecumenical Movement," *Shane Quarterly* 15 (1954), 16–20.

recognition of members in one Baptism, (3) mutual recognition of ordained ministry, and (4) mutual recognition that each church affirms the apostolic faith of scripture and tradition. The remaining marks were actions that would draw the separate churches into closer relations with one another: (5) provide for celebration of the Eucharist together; (6) engagement together in Christ's mission on a regular and intentional basis, especially to combat racism; (7) intentional commitment to promote unity, giving special attention to marginalization for reasons such as race, age, gender, forms of disability, sexual orientation, and class; (8) an ongoing process of theological dialogue, especially on racism and reconciliation of ministries; and (9) appropriate structures of accountability and appropriate means for consultation and decision making. Discussions at the plenary assembly and thereafter focused primarily on two of these marks: the reconciling of ministries, with issues related to apostolic succession paramount; and overcoming racism, with a conscience-driven rejection of white racism, as the constant point of reference.

Soon thereafter, Kinnamon concluded that the Episcopal Church would not enter the new relationship if reconciliation of ordained ministries remained on the list of visible marks. COCU's executive committee revised the list by removing that mark and rearranging the remaining eight so that the ongoing process of theological dialogue would conclude the list. Their hope was that a way to reconcile the separated ministries could be developed within the context of this ongoing theological discussion. COCU leaders decided that the transformation of COCU into CUIC would take place in a liturgy of word and sacrament in which the churches would confess the sin of division and ask for healing and reconciliation. They would also demonstrate their commitment to work for justice and mercy in the world around them.

As COCU's commission on worship was no longer meeting, I kept abreast of these actions primarily through the reports that continued to be published in *Mid-Stream*. My direct engagement picked up again when I was invited to chair the committee to draft the liturgies by which COCU would terminate its work and CUIC would be established to continue the commission to draw these churches together in closer unity of faith, sacramental life, and mission in Christ's name to people everywhere. Although much of our work was done by correspondence, the important decisions were made in meetings when committee members were present in person. We drew on earlier liturgies that COCU commissions and committees had created but revised them in keeping with the new actions that these liturgies would bring about.

On January 19, 2002, a congregation of approximately 600 crowded into St. Mary's Episcopal Cathedral in Memphis, Tennessee, to mark the ending of COCU's forty-year life. The eucharistic liturgy that COCU had published in 1968 was the basis for this concluding act of worship. The next afternoon, an even larger congregation, perhaps as many as 1,000 congregants, gathered at Mt. Olive Cathedral of the Christian Methodist Episcopal Church for a service of word and sacrament that inaugurated Churches Uniting in Christ. The next day delegates to the unity events joined citizens of Memphis in a procession from City Hall to the Lorraine Motel, which had become the National Civil Rights Museum, to commemorate Martin Luther King Jr., who had been assassinated at that location thirty-four years earlier.

I was grateful for the privilege of working one last time with leaders of Protestant churches at the center of American life, with Christian unity as our central focus. At the same time, I was disappointed and discouraged because so many of COCU's central purposes seemed as far from resolution as they had been when COCU had begun. As I later reflected on the Memphis events, back home in the brightness of Arizona's springtime sun, I developed a more hopeful frame of mind concerning the movement for Christian unity at the beginning of a new millennium. One of my longtime habits has been to make lists of ideas, some of which are later expanded into full essays. Following the Memphis convocation, I made three lists that were subsequently fleshed out and published in an issue of *Mid-Stream* devoted exclusively to the Memphis events.[3]

The first list itemized developments that were "tipping the balance toward hope." First was the decision of the major Lutheran Church in this country to participate more fully enriched the ecclesial stream that was now working on issues of unity and mission.

---

[3] Keith Watkins, "Coming Away with Hope: Thoughts about the Inaugural in Memphis of Churches Uniting in Christ." *Mid-Stream* 41 (April/August 2002), 106–107.

Second, the Presbyterian and Episcopal Churches had committed themselves to a bilateral dialogue seeking to resolve the issue of the historic episcopate (which Eugene Carson Blake had described as the "Gordian knot" that kept the churches divided from one another) on behalf of all the COCU churches. Third, the churches were making progress in overcoming two historical challenges: the exclusion of women from leadership, and racism, which separated the churches because of ethnicity and racial differences. A fourth factor, perhaps less evident than the others, was the interest in CUIC that was shown by the small number of young seminarians in attendance at the convocation.

A second set of four factors, in this reflection was that that these developments confirmed my hope that participating churches would continue to represent the American mainstream. First, they continued the tradition of American liberal theology, holding positions that were poised between firmly fixed traditions inherited from the past and ideas that were emerging in the new secularism. Second, these churches were continuing the classic patterns of Christian worship that focused primarily on pulpit, font, and table. Third, links with the Western Catholic Church, already well-established, were growing stronger. Fourth, these churches understood that their ministries and missions should be directed toward the major issues and institutions of American life.

One more set of reflections stated in this essay discussed matters requiring more thought and prayer. Perhaps it ought not be surprising that with six items, this list was the longest of the three. First, "ancient wounds continue to generate pathogens in the bloodstream." A church historian offered "ancient and bloody battles" over "corporate and personal forms of episcopal oversight" as an example. Second, "Short-term memory is, in fact, very short." The example that was mentioned during the discussions was that some delegates had skewed memories of the basic principles that had shaped the Consultation during its founding years. Third, "It is difficult to distinguish between rite, reason, and routine," and as a result theological discussions easily become confused. Fourth, "The churches in CUIC, with their base in the sixteenth-century Reformation, are increasingly separated from the rapidly growing churches with a base in the revivalist or charismatic movements." Fifth, "The status of the mainstream church in American life is greatly diminished." And sixth, "The strong focus on racism obscures the continuing challenge of other problems."

At the time of these activities in Memphis I was seventy years old and had been retired from my professorship for seven years. My direct participation in organizations and processes focused on Christian unity ended at this time. My interest in Christian unity, however, continued, and led me to begin gathering materials and making plans for writing a history of the Consultation on Church Union. During the intervening years my three-fold sense of self—historian, bicyclist, and environmentalist—would continue, but from my back-home-again location in the Pacific Northwest and with revised areas of interest. During these years, I wrote and published two books, unrelated to Christian unity, and explored other issues related to the mission and well-being of protestant churches in the United States.

Independent Historian

In the spring of 1999, two years after the Sun City West actions that established full communion of Lutheran and Reformed Churches, I was planning a solo bicycle journey from San Diego to St. Augustine, a trip of about 3,600 miles that would take about six weeks. At Rotary the previous week, I had given a resumé of my plans. As I returned to my place at the table, a fellow Rotarian, with a look of disbelief on his face, greeted me with a single question: "Why?" It soon became clear, from the look on his face, that he was not persuaded by my response. Even so, he offered to arrange overnight accommodations for me with his daughter and family in San Antonio. A day before flying to San Diego to begin the ride, I sent details to my children and a little later one of them phoned me with deep anxiety in her voice: "Dad! You can't do this. You're sixty-seven years old!" Part of my response was to reassure the kids that their mother was fully acquainted and content that my plans were reasonable and that they didn't need to worry. I chose not to add to their anxiety by telling them that I was not following established bike routes but instead was working my way from one natural or historical landmark that I wanted to see to another. Although there were a few anxious moments, such as two nights when I came close to sleeping on the bare ground because I could find no lodging or shelter, the trip was a highlight of that period of my life.

Sundays were rest days during my bicycle journeys and my church going along the way enriched my experiences of the wide range of liturgical forms. In the Southwestern regions, much of this new learning was related to historical cultural traditions that were new to me. Beginning in southeastern Arizona and continuing into Louisiana, I found myself intersecting a bicycle touring group of about twenty-five women, some of them close to my age. Although I was traveling more miles per day than they, their route was more direct than mine, which explains why we met from time to time.

One evening midway through the journey, I talked by phone with a member of the personnel committee of First Christian Church in Portland, Oregon, who invited me to consider serving as interim minister at her church beginning late in the summer. We continued the discussion by phone and while I was somewhere in central Texas came to an agreement. Billie and I moved temporarily to an apartment on the campus of Portland State University within easy walking distance of the church, and I began my work. I had been acquainted with First Christian Church since the spring of 1948, when I met with its pastor, Myron C. Cole, at the urging of my class advisor at nearby Lincoln High School, to seek his guidance on college plans. Although I often walked past the church on my way downtown after the school day was over, this was my first and only visit until many years later, when Billie and I attended worship there during Portland visits. In the 1970s, my mother had become a member there but had been unable to attend during her final years of life. Despite these contacts, I knew little about the congregation.

Wayne Bryant, who had been pastor for seventeen years, was retiring and would be serving as interim regional minister in Oregon. He was an engaging preacher, a skilled organizer of congregational life, and an active leader in the life of the city. We had talked occasionally over the years, and I had a positive regard for his pastoral insights and skills. I had read extensively in literature about interim ministries, attended workshops on the subject, and talked extensively with friends who were experienced in doing that kind of work, all of which gave me a strong set of ideas about how to do the work. A skilled office staff and corps of volunteers were in place, and I moved quickly into a pattern of work, focusing attention on keeping things going in their accustomed ways, suggesting revisions in program and worship from time to time, and engaging in pastoral care as needed. During my time at First Christian, I learned about the significant ministries of Thompson L. Shannon, Myron C. Cole, and Harold Glen Brown from 1939 through 1966. I became aware of the fact that one of the congregation's elders, Stephen E. Epler, had established an extension program for veterans coming home from World War II, which was to become Portland State University in the South Park Blocks, just up the street from First Christian.

I also became interested in the histories of the downtown Portland churches. Even though Portland has been one of the least observant cities in the nation, the old First Churches, with one exception, had remained as relatively vigorous congregations on sites they had occupied for a century and longer. Even First United Methodist Church—which, following World War II, moved from its historic site—had relocated on a new site in a historic neighborhood close to the central city. I visited the pastors of these churches, toured their buildings, and wrote brief notes about their congregations, filing them away for further reference. Although this legacy is one that still interests me, the time has passed for me to write even a respectable research essay on this topic. During these same months, I also became convinced that a history of First Christian Church would be worth doing and made initial explorations in the church's archives, which were extensive and well arranged. Although this project was more interesting and seemed more possible to accomplish, it too had to be postponed until another time.

A major reason for the delay was that I was devoting as much time as possible to completing my history of Christian Theological Seminary. The primary source of documents and data was the archival collection at the seminary, especially the papers of Frederick D. Kershner, the founding dean of the College of Religion at Butler University. Before moving from Indianapolis and during family visits after our move to the West, I spent long hours going through this vast array of papers, taking notes and making copies. I traveled to several cities in Indiana and adjacent states to interview people who had been part of the story in earlier years. J. Irwin Miller, whose family had for generations been patrons of Butler University and the seminary, provided access to papers in his family's archives. I read minutes of trustee and faculty meetings and engaged my colleagues in occasional conversations. As portions of the manuscript took shape, I asked some of my former seminary colleagues to review and comment, and I revised as seemed appropriate. As the manuscript was nearing completion, I became aware of Guild Press of Indiana, a small publishing company that was owned and operated by a woman who had previously been a professor of English at Butler University. She reviewed the manuscript and indicated her readiness to publish it. The copy editor who covered my manuscript with blue comments and corrections was especially interested because she and Ronald Osborn's daughter had been close friends at Shortridge High School.

While we still were in Portland, I sent the completed manuscript to the seminary's new president, whom I did not know, for review and comment, and then made a trip to Indianapolis to discuss it in person. During that conversation it became clear that the ownership of the manuscript needed to be clarified. Back in Portland I consulted a lawyer specializing in copyright law who, after reading my correspondence and records, rendered the opinion that I owned the manuscript and had full right to publish. With this question answered, I completed my work and sent a copy of the revised manuscript to J. Irwin Miller, then 91 years of age, in the hope that he would read it and comment. During my next trip to Indianapolis, he invited me to his home in Columbus for lunch and conversation about the manuscript. He commended my way of laying out facts in an orderly way, leaving it to readers to draw their own conclusions about the actions that were taken.

CTS President Richard D. N. Dickinson Jr. had offered me an honorarium of $500 for writing the book, which I received in installments. Guild Press published it without requiring me to pay any part of the editorial costs. As the book was being designed, however, the press offered to do the jacket in full color if I would pay the five-hundred-dollar cost of this upgrade, which I gladly did. The result is a beautiful, hardcover book based on thorough research of primary documents. I made special efforts to keep my own involvements in the seminary's history in proper balance. Even so, the book has autobiographical undertones because it tells the story of an institution that has been a basic part of my life and has done much to make me the person, pastor, and scholar I have become. It was published in 2001.

In many ways I enjoyed my work as interim pastor at First Christian Church. Even so, I began feeling depression that was similar to what I had experienced while developing Mesa de Cristo. After eight months with the Portland congregation, we returned to Arizona and a second person continued the interim ministry. But this time in Portland confirmed the conclusion that had already been forming, that we would sell our home in Sun City West and move back to the Pacific Northwest. The move was in two stages, the first being another eight-month interim ministry, this one at First Christian Church in Albany, Oregon. Our Arizona house sold just in time, and we moved everything north, living the first six months in a house we leased from longtime members of the congregation who were moving to a retirement community. During the first part of our time in Albany, we made biweekly house-hunting trips to Portland which resulted in our buying a condominium in Vancouver, Washington, just across the Columbia River from Portland.

After my time in Albany closed and we were fully moved, we joined First Christian Church in Portland and reestablished our basic patterns of life. For me, this meant reading and writing on religious topics and bicycling around the Pacific Northwest. At the request of the regional minister, I agreed to do two short term-interim ministries, each one for a four-month term. The first was in Hood River, Oregon, which provided the opportunity of becoming better acquainted with one of the most distinctive communities in the region. The other was at First Christian Church in Salem, which enjoyed the largest attendance of any Disciples congregation in Oregon.

As time allowed, I pushed forward with my research into the history of First Christian Church in Portland. In 2003, I completed a draft history of more than 200 pages with the title, "Liberal-Minded Religion in a Downtown Church." After a cursory summary of the church's first half-century, the manuscript describes the congregation's life beginning in 1939, when Thompson L. Shannon became pastor, and concluding with the major renovation of its seventy-year-old building in 1984. The final chapter, "Liberal Evangelicalism," is a statement of why churches did so well during the "brief golden age," which is a major part of the story the manuscript depicts. I sent copies of the manuscript to a short list of persons, two or three members of the congregation, and others to professional colleagues. Only one person—Paul A. Crow Jr., himself a church historian —responded. He returned my draft with many notes, questions, and suggestions. Although I believed in the project and was confident that with careful revision it would be a solid contribution to the historical record, I hesitated to do it. Parts of the story were painful, and some of the participants were still active in the church.

My one effort to tell the church's story to congregants was in the summer of 2005, after becoming a member of the congregation, when I wrote and presented four lectures during the adult forum on Sunday mornings. As the title of the series, "Disciples Who Have Influenced the Nation," indicates, the lectures were national in scope but localized in focus. I sketched the influence of Charles Clayton Morrison, longtime editor of the *Christian Century*, which for more than a century has been the voice of progressive Protestant churches. I interpreted the impact of three Disciples who have served as president of the United States: James A. Garfield, Lyndon Johnson, and Ronald Reagan. I devoted one of the lectures to J. Irwin Miller. In the final presentation, under the title "Progressive Religion at First Christian Church," I outlined the work of two of its members of previous years: Paul J. Raver, who was the first full-time administrator of Bonneville Power Administration, and Edith Green, who many years later was recognized as one of the most influential members of the U.S. House of Representatives.

In 2009, I delivered a précis of this story as the Kirkpatrick Lecture, sponsored by the Disciples of Christ Historical Society. The title of the lecture was, "Religion Becoming Public Service: A Chapter in the Life of First Christian Church, Portland, Oregon." My explanation for this topic was that the general history of this period in American church life was well known, but the stories of congregations were not. This local history provided some of the details of how the changes developed in specific places. Except for the Kirkpatrick Lecture, all of this research and writing about First Christian Church in Portland remains unpublished. In the summer of 2008, Laurie Pratt retired from his position as minister of music and organist at First Christian Church, a post he had held for fifty-six years. In order to honor Laurie and his work and to preserve this part of the story, I wrote a carefully researched essay entitled, "Nurturing an Informed Spirituality: Reflections upon the Music Ministry of Laurie Pratt."

Another writing project took shape following a work-study seminar at the Yakama Christian Mission in White Swan,

Washington.[4] My wife and I were part of a larger group of older adults from First Christian Church who spent several days working and talking with people at the Mission Church and at the JustLiving Farm, where the mission director, David Bell, lived and conducted some of the mission's major activities. I discovered that no history of this century-old ministry had been written and that many of the records had been destroyed when several homes were leveled in a brush fire. In order to write a short history, I sought out written materials from various sources and conducted interviews with a short list of people who have been active in the life of the mission. The Disciples of Christ Historical Society offered to publish the book as one of the first volumes of its new publishing arm, Polar Star Press. The society's staff enhanced the manuscript by commissioning (without my knowledge) a very good foreword by Loretta Hunnicut, a historian at Pepperdine University, and selecting photographs from the Society's holdings and interspersing them throughout the book. It was published in 2009 with the title *A Visible Sign of God's Presence: A History of the Yakama Christian Mission*.

I am glad to have written this book, but I regret that I did not delve more deeply into historical and theological issues, including the "doctrine of discovery" that David Bell in recent years has been calling to the attention of our church. In a conversation at the 2017 General Assembly of the Christian Church (Disciples of Christ), Bell acknowledged that the book tells only part of the story, but he affirmed that even as it stands, the book is useful because it is the sole public record of the mission's history. At the time of our discussion, eight years after the book's publication, it was still listed on Amazon: "By sketching out the long view of Yakama Christian Mission's past," the one customer review stated, "Watkins invites us into the long view of the mission's future, a value that the current staff continues to promote. The hope is, writes Watkins, in programs that can empower current youth so that future families will be educated, healthy and whole." Two used copies were available at $54.99, and the book was ranked at 6,540,062 on Amazon's list of bestsellers. In recent years, significant books about the Yakama people have been published,

---

[4] Yakama is the original spelling of the reservation's name and is still used by the tribal government and by the Yakama Christian Mission.

including *Yakama Rising: Indigenous Cultural Revitalization, Activism, and Healing*, by Michelle M. Jacob.[5]

The American Church that Might Have Been

The active life of the Consultation on Church Union ended in Memphis because the churches had long since lost interest in the model of Christian unity that the Consultation had advocated. The stalwart church leaders who had given the project energy—people like Eugene Carson Blake (Presbyterian), Robert F. Gibson Jr. (Episcopalian), W. Clyde Williams (Christian Methodist Episcopal), and Paul A. Crow Jr. (Disciples)—had died or were no longer active. The published documents were, for the most part, available in *Mid-Stream*, which was an obscure theological quarterly, or in pamphlets that easily get lost on library shelves. Personal papers of some of the major participants were gradually making their way into archival deposits, and COCU's official papers were deposited in a special collection at the Princeton Theological Seminary Library. Although I still owned most of the pamphlets and major documents, my papers were fragmentary and my memories were fading.

Three factors, however, gave me reason to believe that I could write this history. One was that I had followed it from the beginning and participated in significant fashion for most of its history. Another reason was that I had strong continuing relations with some of COCU's prominent figures, especially Paul Crow, who had been at its center successively as associate general secretary, first full-time executive secretary, and head of the Disciples delegation from 1963 until COCU's closing. Some of the relevant issues of *Mid-Stream* remained in my personal library, and my travels took me frequently to theological libraries where I had access to this journal. Increasingly, documents of this type were becoming available on electronic databases. Some of the people with whom I had worked were still available for comment and advice.

I believed in the vision that COCU embodied and earnestly desired that this new church would come into being. I embraced the widening of its mission when social factors such as racism were redefined as theological issues equal in importance to classic theological issues such as apostolic succession. One of my deepest disappointments was the realization that none of the participating

---

[5] Tucson, AZ: University of Arizona Press, 2013.

churches, including my own, had been willing to reform its internal operations in order to become more like the new American Protestant church we had thought would be capable of serving the kind of nation that the United States was becoming. By writing this book, I could weave the scattered records, memories, actions, and actors into a unified and coherent story. I had no illusions about the impact this book might have. Few people would buy it, and the best I could hope for was that it would find a place in theological libraries and electronic databases.

As the manuscript neared completion, Michael Kinnamon was appointed to a position as visiting professor at Seattle University, and we made it a practice to meet for conversation each time I was in the city visiting my family. We talked about the book as it was taking shape, and after reviewing the manuscript, he responded favorably to my request that he write an introduction to the book. He offered to write to a senior editor at Eerdmans Publishing, with whom he had worked on other projects, asking if that company would be interested in seeing the manuscript. The editor's response was that he was willing to look at it, but he warned Michael that their readers showed little interest in "old-style ecumenism," and therefore it was not likely that his company would be interested in publishing it.

Following the lead of two of my former colleagues at the seminary, I sent a proposal and sample chapter to Wipf and Stock, an innovative and active publisher of religious books, based in Eugene, Oregon. Two weeks later, I received a positive response. They would accept the manuscript as soon as it was ready and publish it under their Pickwick Publications imprint. I was overjoyed by their decision. Even though the book would likely attract a limited readership, a major purpose in writing it would have been achieved. COCU's basic story had been drawn together in one sustained narrative that would henceforth be available to church leaders, scholars, and the denominations.

During the final few weeks of finishing up the manuscript, I was especially grateful for the help that Billie gave me. Although she was in the late stages of treatment for cancer, she continued to read my materials as I wrote them. She rarely commented on the ideas I was unfolding, but she called attention to obscure sentences, questionable grammar, misspelled words, and punctuation that needed fixing. She died while the manuscript was at the publishers.

When I came home after the trip to Indianapolis for her last rites, the electronic file with the complete manuscript was waiting for me to proof one more time. The book, which was published later that year (2014), begins with the dedication:

> Remembering with love, Billie Lee Caton Watkins
> Now singing alto in the Choir of Angels
> July 19, 1931—August 12, 2014.

Although most of this book describes the labors of people other than myself, it cannot help but be, in some significant sense, a memoir of my own professional life. This personal dimension is most clearly evident in the final two chapters. In the chapter titled, "Remembering the Church that Never Came to Be," I summarize what the COCU churches tried to do, give reasons why the venture had seemed so promising, explain why it lost momentum, and summarize the achievements. "If one conclusion can be derived from this history," I write, "it is that the century-long pursuit of multilateral church mergers can no longer be regarded as an effective way to achieve Christian unity in the United States. It is hard to imagine any combination of theological or social factors, save the virtual collapse of existing ecclesial systems, that could inspire a new effort to achieve a comprehensive American plan of church union in the decades immediately before us."[6]

Later in the chapter I summarize my understanding of COCU's achievements. My first conclusion, following the lead of historian David A. Hollinger, is that the ecumenical Protestant churches (as Hollingsworth refers to them) were culture changers and that the Consultation was one of the instruments they used to respond creatively to challenges the nation and its churches were facing. Another conclusion is that the Consultation served as a laboratory for testing some of the ideas and practices that were vigorously promoted among the churches. Some of these ideas were coming from academicians and activists who were calling for a dramatic reshaping of ecclesial systems, and COCU's efforts to put them into practice were providing some of the feedback that was needed to evaluate their feasibility. Still another contribution this movement

---

[6] Keith Watkins, *The American Church that Might Have Been: A History of the Consultation on Church Union* (Eugene, OR: Wipf and Stock, 2015), 182.

for union made was that it created a theological consensus that could guide the churches into a way of life that would make them more complete than they could hope to be if they were to maintain their existing patterns of belief and practice. COCU also demonstrated the difference between voluntary cooperation and binding commitment in bringing about institutional change. Binding commitments, such as those brought about by institutional merger, make it difficult to back out when the challenges increase. Instead, churches have to stay together until something new emerges. A final conclusion on my list in the book is that discussion during these forty years of close connection contributed to the ongoing discussion concerning the relationship of religion and culture.

It ought not be a surprise that the book's final chapter, only five pages in length, bears the title "Still Needed—A New Church for a New Nation." After describing the significant changes taking place in American life and referring even more briefly to ideas coming from new visionaries, I state this conviction:

> [T]he churches that trace their heritage to the Reformation inspired by Luther, Calvin, Cranmer, and others have a continuing role in American life. These churches seek to order their lives so that they are faithful to the past, attentive to the present, and oriented toward a future that is consistent with the Holy Commonwealth that Jesus proclaimed. The need for this kind of historic Protestant presence in this post-Christendom era is intensified by the fact that strident, politically and culturally conservative versions of church-sponsored activity have become such a dominant and divisive force in public affairs.[7]

The churches that were part of the Consultation need to continue their emphasis on modeling the new humanity in all aspects of their worship, congregational life, and mission. Social status, gender, race and ethnicity, and nationality should no longer divide us because all members are "one in Christ." This means, in part, that programs to combat racism will continue to be central to the Protestantism that the nation needs. The historic protestant readiness to embrace learning and follow in ways that are consistent with science, history,

---

[7] Keith Watkins, *The American Church that Might Have Been*, 198.

and philosophy needs to continue as an active element in the Protestant church that the nation needs. One place where this kind of witness is especially important pertains to the rapidly increasing threat of climate change.

One more conclusion needs to be stated. The kind of churchly presence that COCU envisioned will seek to attend to the soul of the nation in which it "lives and moves and has its being." Religion and society inevitably are intertwined, and the results are sometimes destructive to one or both of these entities. Even so, the relationship continues, and the religious emphasis shapes much of what a society and its leaders do. Although several religious traditions have shaped this nation in the past, and other traditions are now joining in the mix, the ecumenical Protestant churches have historically made the strongest contribution, for good or ill. The work must go on, and the long experience and general orientation of these churches will continue to be essential for the well-being of the nation.

Two years after publication of *The American Church that Might Have Been*, the Consultation on Church Union came again to the forefront of my work docket. I was invited to present "an inspiring address" recounting COCU's history at a convocation of Churches Uniting in Christ that would take place at Christian Chapel Temple of Faith Christian Methodist Episcopal Church in Dallas, Texas, on Pentecost Sunday, June 4, 2017. Since the guidelines given to me were sketchy, I decided to write a paper suitable for a scholarly conference and adapt it as needed when I received more details. The manuscript that emerged was a precis of my 225-page COCU history, with a concluding section adapted to the Dallas convocation. The manuscript was nearing completion when further details concerning the event arrived in the mail. It was described as "a national celebration of the member churches' recognition of the ordained ministries of each communion and a celebration of the Eucharist at one common table of the Lord." Scheduled for the preceding afternoon was a forum on race and reconciliation. These events would take place at the host church, which was located near the Galleria, a major retail and commercial complex in North Dallas.

The Sunday afternoon assembly, I learned after arriving in Dallas, was described as a worship service, planned to take two hours. It included an extended litany, interpretive remarks by CUIC leaders, a choir anthem, prayers, and the celebration of the Eucharist.

My presentation was listed as a sermon, one of three that would be proclaimed during the service. The two other preachers were African Americans, who delivered tightly structured sermons in Black homiletical style. The service took half an hour longer than projected. Although I have not seen a time report, my hunch is that I, the White preacher, had the longest sermon of the afternoon, even though I omitted most of the historical account of COCU's life that was in my manuscript.

As I prepared this address, I came to a deeper appreciation of COCU's sixteenth plenary assembly years at Baltimore, November 26–30, 1984, thirty-three years prior to the Dallas consultation: This was the turning point in the Consultation's life. Delegates from the nine participating churches approved and recommended to their churches a substantial document entitled *The COCU Consensus: In Quest of a Church of Christ Uniting*. The decisive character of this moment in COCU's history was stated in an address by John Deschner, one of the Consultation's most respected leaders. In his academic life, he was an expert on John Wesley and a professor at Perkins Theological Seminary. He had represented his church on the Commission on Faith and Order of the World Council of Churches, serving as moderator in 1982, when the Commission adopted the convergent text, *Baptism, Eucharist and Ministry*, and had also served as chair of COCU's theology commission. The Consultation was at a turning point in three ways, Deschner declared. First, the churches had shifted from an external ecumenism to an internal ecumenism, from "a COCU-centered to a church-centered next step in the quest for a Church of Christ Uniting." Second, the "way ahead is not a decision of each church about COCU, but about the other churches: does our church recognize the ministries of the other *churches* as apostolic? Does COCU's work help our church acknowledge the other *churches* as 'authentic parts of the One, Holy, Catholic and Apostolic Church of Jesus Christ?" Third, the churches were being asked to adopt a greater degree of seriousness in their relations with one another.

Deschner's statement unwittingly intensified the family metaphor that Martin Marty had introduced into the COCU conversation more than twenty years earlier. Marty had described the churches as cousins seeking to become brothers and sisters. Deschner's metaphor was that COCU had served as a marriage broker for the churches. "It has even drafted out for them how to pop the question. An engagement ring is the next step, and that has to happen between the churches" (p. 152). Four years later, at COCU's seventeenth plenary assembly in New Orleans, December 5-9, 1988, delegates revised their 1984 draft and recommended *In Quest of a Church of Christ Uniting* to their churches.

Near the conclusion of my address, I referred to the family analogy. The COCU churches, I commented, took a decade to develop their formal responses to the plan that would bring them together into a new church that would be truly catholic, truly evangelical, and truly reformed. They prepared serious responses that affirmed many aspects of the plan and expressed a certain readiness to move forward. The reservations were stronger, however, and it became clear that they were not ready to exchange the churches they already knew for a church that did not yet exist. Theological barriers were too high and institutional barriers seemed even more insurmountable. After thirty years of deepening friendship, the churches decided to stay cousins. Becoming brothers and sisters in a new family was more than they could do, and popping the question was inconceivable. When they finally acknowledged that the COCU vision could not be achieved, the churches established a new way to stay together, Churches Uniting in Christ (CUIC). Since then, we have stayed in good relations with one another, but we no longer dream of becoming the new American church that we once believed to be God's will for our ecclesial life.

My somber but hopeful conclusion was that as I traveled among the churches, no longer active in leadership but very much a part of living, worshiping, and ministering congregations, I sensed that our churches have largely settled back into our separate ways of life, bound more by the past than pulled forward by the future. Has any of our churches, I asked, reshaped its faith, ministry, polity, and mission according to ecumenical standards? After more than half a century of relations in COCU and CUIC, some churches cannot live without bishops, other churches cannot live with them, and still others have been finding ways of accommodating the office. Racism continues to be one of the deepest challenges in American life. We participated in the Civil Rights Movement in the 1950s and 1960s. Our churches changed, and we helped the larger society repent of the past and find new ways that no longer were defined by race. At our best, we fell short of the desired goals. In more recent years, institutional racism has reasserted itself, often in new ways and based on new ideas. It is relatively easy to describe what is wrong and how we got this way. Yet evil passions are abroad in the land, and we are having increasing difficulty in deciding how best to respond. No matter what our theology might be, most of us continue to participate in churches where the members look, think, and act the way we do. While our churches have made progress here and there, we have not yet found ways of modeling the new society that we believe God intends.

I concluded with words of gratitude, because most of our churches were readier than they had been in 1960 to exercise eucharistic hospitality to one another, even though we still are still estranged over matters of eucharistic theology, ministerial form, and institutional history. The vision, however, continues, that by sharing in this meal in which our crucified and risen Savior comes to us in his continuing life, we are connected to one another in a new way.

My recollections of the annual meetings of the Consultation on Church Union are that delegates representing the churches and people from the host community would number close to 300. The CUIC convocation in Dallas attracted about a third of that number. One of the benefits for me as a White man was the prominence of Black voices in both the forum on race and the convocation and Eucharist on Sunday. Since we were meeting on the first Sunday of the month, the morning service at Christian Chapel Temple of Faith was the celebration of the Lord's supper. A large congregation came together that morning and a choir of more than fifty voices led worshipers in strong Black gospel music. The church's pastor, Rev. D. Vanessee Burns, preached a strong sermon that combined a skillful development of the biblical text for the morning and an African American style of exposition. The order of worship and the eucharistic liturgy followed a classic Methodist pattern. The combination of ecumenically satisfying liturgical form and vibrant, culturally relevant ceremonial style was one of the high points of my weekend in Dallas.

The weekend illustrated the radical shift in emphasis in the COCU–CUIC approach to Christian unity. Despite the announced purpose of celebrating the mutual recognition of ministries in all the churches, no debate or action on this difficult issue was taken. Instead, the dominant emphasis was on the theme of the Saturday forum on race and reconciliation. As far as I could see, little had changed since COCU's executive committee had removed recognition of ministries from its list and placed the primary emphasis on racial reconciliation.

Changing Course to Follow Our Polar Star

A month after the Dallas convocation of Churches Uniting in Christ, the Christian Church (Disciples of Christ) held its biennial General Assembly in Indianapolis. As I had reestablished my residence in Indianapolis, it was easy for me to participate in the assembly and observe current eucharistic and ecumenical emphases of my own church. The evening event each day was described as worship rather than as a plenary assembly and consisted primarily of congregational singing, prayers, readings from the Bible, and a sermonic address. Each evening program was concluded with a celebration of the Lord's supper. The eucharistic portions were carefully prepared and skillfully led. Although varied in ceremonial detail and using different prayers each evening, the services were devotionally satisfying and ended each day in a manner appropriate for a churchly convention. These General Assembly celebrations confirmed that Disciples, along with the other ecumenical Protestant churches that had gathered in Dallas, continue their traditional ways of doing things, although favorably impacted by the theological ideas and liturgical patterns of the wider Christian world.

One of the strongest features of the assembly, in its general program and its worship, was its highlighting the importance of *wholeness*, the key word that anchored the recently established identity statement of our church: *We are Disciples of Christ, a movement for wholeness in a fragmented world. As part of the one body of Christ we welcome all to the Lord's Table as God has welcomed us.* This theme is extensively developed in a document published in 2017 by the Disciples Council on Christian Unity, with the title, *Called to Live Life in Unity: A Disciples of Christ Ministry for Christian Unity and Unity for All Humanity.* The Council's president, Paul S. Tche, writes that the Council had decided to address four aspects of injustice that currently are dividing the church and the human community: "1) racial injustice; 2) ecological injustice; 3) economic injustice; and 4) international injustice." The Council would "encourage the Disciples and other communions to work together and to put theological and structural differences behind us, not for the sake of the church itself but for the sake of the world in which the church finds its purpose and mission to exist as a faith community."[8] No explanation is given as to what it means "to put theological and structural differences behind us." The Council's document makes no reference to the classic "church-dividing issues," such as doctrines of ministry and ordination, which continue to keep Christians from full communion with one another. The definitive paragraph in the entire document states the matter clearly:

> We honor our heritage as a movement for Christian unity by cooperating and partnering with other Christian communities to work for bringing about wholeness—healing and justice—in the world. This is what it means to be "ecumenical." One example is our partnership with the United Church of Christ for the past 25 years. We also honor the heritage of Christian unity by staying together in covenant as a witness to the world that even when we disagree we can still make room, welcoming all to the table as Christ has welcomed us. Our spiritual ancestors were fond of saying, "unity, not uniformity."[9]

The Disciples' diminishing interest in the classic church-dividing issues is clearly seen in the failure to take part in the one form of putting "theological and structural differences behind us" that is actually taking place today: entering into full communion with other Lutheran and Reformed churches. In an effort to gain perspective on this perplexing state of affairs, I initiated an email conversation with Thomas Best, whom I met when we both were young professors in Indianapolis, I at Christian Theological Seminary and he at Butler University. He referred to Thomas and Alexander Campbell who had had "enough trouble trying to reconcile just Presbyterians in Scotland and Ireland," and then suggested that the Disciples' "commitment to the open table of the Lord has much to do with [our disinterest in formal reconciliation]. ... Why formalize something that we believe Jesus has ordained, and that we practice already?"

---

[8] *Called to Live Life in Unity: A Disciples of Christ Ministry for Christian Unity and Unity for All Humanity* (Indianapolis: Disciples Council on Christian Unity, 2017), 19. Text is available at <https://disciples.org/our-identity/>.

[9] Ibid, 5.

He noted that many Episcopalians "now extend a welcome to the Table to all baptized Christians. ... Perhaps we feel the problem has resolved itself (among Protestants broadly) without the energy, etc. needed for formal agreements."[10]

In response to my question concerning the validity of a Disciples celebration, as viewed by people in other churches, Tom responded that he didn't know, but then continued by saying that it may depend on their attitude to "free" as opposed to "prescribed" prayers, and their readiness to recognize a common "intention" rather than requiring a form of words that looks like theirs. A central issue would be the elders' prayers—not so much for their content (which can always be improved, as we well know), but for the very fact of their being at the table. It is a radical example of the whole people of God being involved in the service, an extension of the priesthood of all believers—there are good grounds for our practice, and my experience is that other churches are intrigued and even, sometimes, attracted by it. He then said that he had

been wrestling with many of these issues as a member of the international Disciples/Roman Catholic Dialogue. It's a different context, since there's no question of full communion, we have such different approaches to ministry, etc. But for what it's worth: the Catholics have experienced Disciples Lord's Supper services in wildly different contexts—from Bethany to big-steeple to Puerto Rico. And they have said: on the level of experience, yes, this is the Lord's Table, and the Lord is there. It is church, it is Eucharist. Where they stumble, or wonder, is on questions of authority and regularity: without a magisterium, how do Disciples know that what they are doing is within the norm? Without a set form of words, how do Disciples know that what is said and done adds up to an authentic eucharist? Perhaps these are the questions which especially Episcopalians and Lutherans would ask in the U.S., if in a milder form.[11]

From the earliest years of our movement's life, Sunday worship has focused on the celebration of the Lord's supper, led by elders chosen from the congregation. Ordinarily, there have been two elders at the communion table, each othering a prayer. The first offered a prayer of thanksgiving for the bread and the second offered a prayer of thanksgiving for the cup. It was common practice to add

---

[10] Email from Tom Best, December 11, 2017.
[11] Ibid.

a phrase, such as "which symbolizes Christ's body broken for us" or "Christ's blood poured out for many." Although this phrasing gives little attention to classic interpretations of the bread and wine as used at the communion table, it does keep the prayers focused on the central actions celebrated when Christians gather for "the breaking of the bread." From the beginning, we were convinced that the elders who led worship would ordinarily offer prayers they had prepared rather than repeat prayers from authorized books of worship. Even this simple reference to the loaf and cup in remembrance of Jesus, however, sometimes would disappear.

During the second half of the nineteenth century, the style of Disciples' worship gradually changed. Congregations around the country moved away from pioneer culture and developed more formal patterns of worship and replaced frontier cabins with architect-designed and -decorated buildings. One of the most important of these new factors was the development of worship manuals and guides to the celebration of the communion service. Although congregational elders continued to offer these prayers, for the most part using their own words, these guides helped them maintain a focus on classic ideas about the meaning of this sacred meal.[12]

My impression as I travel around among Disciples congregations is that leadership by elders chosen from the congregation continues to be the norm in our churches and that, for the most part, they prepare their own texts. Some select prayers from books or guides; some write their prayers before coming to church or as the service or sermon are taking place; and still others pray extemporaneously with no written text or notes in front of them. Although prayers at the table usually make some reference to classic meanings of the Lord's supper, this is not always what happens. Instead, prayers may mention some event or celebration from current events or the secular calendar, with virtually no reference to the meaning of the liturgical eating and drinking that are about to happen. When the words that express the meaning of the actions with the loaf and cup fall short, the service falls short of its spiritual climax and it

---

[12] For a thorough study of this aspect of Disciples history, see Gerard Moore, *The Disciples at the Lord's Table: Prayers Over Bread and Cup Across 150 Years of Christian Church (Disciples of Christ History)* (Eugene, OR: Pickwick Publications, 2015), 30–32.

is likely that worshipers go away with their religious expectations unfulfilled.

When we personalize and secularize the church's most important set of words—the great thanksgiving prayer at the communion table—we are diminishing the central core of our religious life with one another. Although I have told myself on previous occasions that I've done all that I could to help my church fulfill its historical purposes, and therefore I simply should let it go, this still is hard to do.

Instead of Melancholy, Deep Thanksgiving

If I were to stop now, this theological memoir would confirm the observation that longtime COCU colleague Jerry Moede made after reading my reflections written as COCU was becoming CUIC. He detected a sense of melancholy in these meditations about the many years of work I had done trying to bring American churches into a deeper sense of spiritual and organic oneness as we meet together around the eucharistic table. My focus all these years has been on what long has been called organic unity. At this late stage in my work, I am realizing that another kind of separation of people around the world is even more heart-rending, soul-searching, and physically destructive than the ecclesial separations that have prompted so many of our efforts to establish Christian unity. It is the worldwide separation of people from one another as we all face the never-ending struggle to become whole, both as persons one by one and as communities here and everywhere. The emerging center of the work of churches around the world is the committing of ourselves and our churches to the tasks of uniting all of humanity so that we are bound together into the kind of well-being that God has intended from the very beginning.

This, then, may be the new work that God is giving me to do: *to focus attention on the transformed understanding of unity that now is at the center of Disciples' statements of meaning, and to develop suggestions about eucharistic practice and ecclesial form that will help congregations everywhere use unity around Christ's table as the basis for working for healing and wholeness in the full range of human life.* In recent years, many of my colleagues, friends, and family members have already come to this understanding and now lead the way.

Not least of them is my daughter, Sharon E. Watkins, who from 2005 through 2017 served as general minister and president of the Christian Church (Disciples of Christ) in the United States and Canada. In the introduction to her book, *Whole: A Call to Unity in Our Fragmented World*, she describes a process by which Disciples developed our current understanding of who we are at this time in history. It began in 2005 when, as her first act in her new office, she sought to enlist 10,000 Disciples from across the land to be daily prayer partners in this venture. Then came a visioning team, a small group of people "who could help the Church begin thinking about where we found ourselves at that precise moment and where God might be calling us next."[13] The team would work with a recently issued mission statement that had already been incorporated into a document called the "2020 Vision," which provided succinct statements of the Disciples' mission and vision.

But the 21st Century Vision Team, Sharon continues, "felt strongly that there was a prior question to answer. That Question was, Who are we? Why is there a Christian Church (Disciples of Christ) at all? Within the whole family of God, what is our particular Disciples identity?" After stating that this church emerged as "a Christian unity movement," and the underlying conviction that shaped this emphasis was that "a united church would offer a contagious witness to the world," the Team reached the conclusion that "our core historical value [is] unity for the sake of the world." It then stated that the term *unity* "has lost luster through its association with the specific and now dated unity efforts of previous generations" and now needs to be replaced with a way "to state our conviction that would work for twenty-first-century Christians."

The statement that was developed during her first term as general minister and president and now is used throughout the church is this: *We are Disciples of Christ, a movement for wholeness in a fragmented world. As part of the one body of Christ, we welcome all to the Lord's Table as God has welcomed us.*[14] At Sharon's request, I read and commented on the manuscript as it developed. In addition to serving, she too had been active in national leadership with strong, continuing connections to a wide range of religious

---

[13] This section draws on Sharon E. Watkins, *Whole: A Call to Unity in Our Fragmented World* (St. Louis: Chalice Press, 2014).

[14] Cited in Sharon Watkins, *Whole*, 3–5.

leaders. In addition to serving as general minister and president, she established important ties to major figures in the nation's cultural and political life, including newly elected President Barack Obama. It was only right that she was even more deeply intertwined with the struggles of her own generation than I had been with mine. One result was that as I worked my way through her book, I sometimes found myself making suggestions that would have brought her closer to positions that represented ideas from my generation, the era that rapidly was disappearing, than to those of her generation. Time and again, however, she held a steady hand as she revised. Whereas the unity for which I had labored had focused on healing communities of faith, the church bodies, so that they could live and minister together harmoniously, the unity to which she was devoting her energies focused on the members of those communities and all others besides, so that, hand in hand, we could all be brought into the loving embrace of God and be made whole.

While tightly connected, these two modes of unity are distinctly different. One focuses attention on healing the ministering communities, the other on healing the entities that are suffering and need to be made whole. Page after page, Sharon provides illustrations of individuals, congregations, and other ecclesial systems that are bringing unity by establishing wholeness. The best way I can resolve this seeming conflict is to say that the unity for which I labored so many years set the stage that helps make it possible for people of this new generation to accomplish the wholeness of life in the world, which is the form that unity is taking now.

At this stage of my life, as my life span is moving toward its completion, I do experience disappointment because some of what I worked for so many years has either not come to pass or fallen short of our generation's hopes. But even stronger is the continuing sense of great joy. Year after year, I shared my energies with a host of earnest, deeply Christian workers. These were the years in which Vatican Two brought the Roman Catholic Church into a new and fruitful interaction with other ecclesial bodies and with contemporary culture while the liturgical movement provided the framework by which Protestant systems around the world entered newly harmonious ways of praying and working together in their ministries for the life of the world. In virtually all of the churchly settings where I find myself these many years later, the theological language, prayer books, hymnals, Bible translations, interchurch relations, and ideas about church and society show signs that they have been shaped by church people with whom I too worked for so many years. And for them I can only offer my deepest thanksgiving. This is a very good time to remember and cling to the prayer from *A New Zealand Prayer Book: He Karakia Mihinare O Aotearoa* that I used during the time I devoted my energies to developing the short-lived Mesa de Cristo Christian Church in Arizona:

> God, give me work, till my life shall end
> And life, till my work is done.[15]

---

[15] *New Zealand Prayer Book* (London: Collins Liturgical Publications, 1997), 125.

Bibliography

Abba, Raymond. *Principles of Christian Worship.* New York: Oxford University Press, 1957.

Adams, Harry Baker. "Worship Among Disciples of Christ, 1865-1920." *Mid-Stream* 7, no. 4 (Summer 1968): 334-339.

Anderson, James D. and Ezra Earl Jones. *The Management of Ministry: Leadership, Purpose, Structure, Community.* San Francisco: Harper & Row, 1978.

Baillie, D. M. Baillie. *God Was in Christ: An Essay on Incarnation and Atonement.* New York: Scribner, 1948.

Barna, George. *User Friendly Churches: What Christians Need to Know About the Churches People Love to Go to.* Ventura, CA: Regal Books, 1991.

Best, Thomas F. "Disciples Identity, Ecumenical Partnership, and the Wider Ecumenical Future." *Mid-Stream* 32, no. 3 (July 1993): 9-27.

_____. Email from Tom Best, December 11, 2017.

Blakemore, W. B. "Worship Among Disciples of Christ, 1920—1966." *Mid-Stream* 7, no. 4 (Summer 1968): 50-65.

Bloy, Myron B. (ed.). *Multi-Media Worship: A Model and Nine Viewpoints.* New York: Seabury Press, 1969.

Brilioth. Yngve. *Eucharistic Faith and Practice: Evangelical and Catholic.* London, UK: SPCK, 1930.

Burt, Robert L. (ed.). *Good News in Growing Churches.* New York: The Pilgrim Press, 1992.

Called to Live Life in Unity: A Disciples of Christ Ministry for Christian Unity and Unity for All Humanity. Indianapolis: Disciples Council on Christian Unity, 2017. (Text is available at *https://disciples.org/our-identity*).

Campbell, Alexander. *A Connected View of the Principles and Rules by which the Living Oracles May Be Intelligently and Certainly Interpreted.* Bethany, WV: McVay and Ewing, 1835.

Cartwright, Colbert S. *Candles of Grace: Disciples Worship in Perspective.* St. Louis: Chalice Press, 1992.

_____. *People of the Chalice: Disciples of Christ in Faith and Practice.* St. Louis: Chalice Press, 1987.

Cartwright, Colbert S., and O. I. Cricket Harrison (eds.). *Chalice Worship.* St. Louis: Chalice Press, 1997.

Chalice Hymnal, edited by Daniel Merrick. St. Louis: Chalice Press, 1995.

Chaney, Charles L. *Church Planting at the End of the Twentieth Century.* Wheaton, IL: Tyndale House, 1991.

Consultation on Church Union. *Principles of Church Union, Guidelines for Structure, and a Study Guide.* Cincinnati: Forward Movement Publications, 1967.

_____. *An Order for the Celebration of Holy Baptism with Commentary.* Cincinnati: Forward Movement Publications, 1973.

_____. *Plan of Union for the Church of Christ Uniting.* Princeton, NJ: Consultation on Church Union, 1970.

Cotton, John. *A Modest and Cleare Answer to Mr. Ball's Discourse of Set Forms of Prayer.* London, U.K. Printed for H. Overton in Popes-Head Alley, 1642.

Council on Christian Unity. *In Spirit and with Honesty.* St. Louis: Christian Board of Publication, 1973.

Council on Christian Unity. *Ordination Service and Guidelines for Ordination for the Christian Church (Disciples of Christ).* Indianapolis: Council on Christian Unity and Homeland Ministries, 1990.

Crow, Paul A., Jr. "Ecumenical Lessons from COCU's History, 1960–1995." *Mid-Stream* 34, no. 3 (July/August 1995): 13–14.

Davies, J. G., G. F. Cope, and D. A. Tyler. *An Experimental Liturgy.* Richmond, VA: John Knox Press, 1958.

Demerath, N.J. III, and Rhys H. Williams. *A Bridging of Faiths: Religion and Politics in a New England City.* Princeton, NJ: Princeton University Press, 1992.

Division of Homeland Ministries. Christian Church (Disciples of Christ). *Worship in the Christian Church: The Common Worship of the Church.* St. Louis: Christian Board of Publication, 1969.

Dix, Gregory. *The Shape of the Liturgy.* London, UK: Dacre Press, Adam & Charles Black, 1945.

Dornhecker, Douglas. "Chalice Worship: How Goes the Reformation?" Paper presented at the Northwest Association for Theological Discussion, February 3–5, 1998.

Drucker, Peter. *The Effective Executive.* New York: Harper & Row, 1966, 1967.

Findlay, John M. "Sun City, Arizona: New Town for Old Folks." In *Magic Lands: Western Cityscapes and American Culture*

After 1940. Berkeley, CA: University of California Press, 1992.
George, Carl F. *Leading and Managing Your Church.* Old Tappan, NJ: Fleming H. Revell, 1987.
Gilkey, Langdon. *How the Church Can Minister to the World Without Losing Itself.* New York: Harper & Row, 1964.
Hadaway, C. Kirk, and David A. Roozen. *Rerouting the Protestant Mainstream: Sources of Growth and Opportunities for Change.* Nashville, TN: Abingdon Press, 1995.
Hadden, Jeffrey K. *The Gathering Storm in the Churches.* Garden City, NY: Doubleday, 1969.
Harris, John C. *Stress, Power, and Ministry: An Approach to the Current Dilemmas of Pastors and Congregations.* Washington, DC: The Alban Institute, 1977.
Hebert, A. G. *Liturgy and Society: The Function of the Church in the Modern World.* London, UK: Faber and Faber, 1956.
Hertzog, Frederick, "The Norm and Freedom of Christian Worship." In *Worship in Scripture and Tradition,* edited by Massey H. Shepherd Jr., 98–127. New York: Oxford University Press, 1963.
Hymnbook for Christian Worship, edited by Charles Huddleston Heaton. St. Louis: Bethany Press, 1970.
In Quest of a Church of Christ Uniting: Called to Live Life in Unity: A Disciples of Christ Ministry for Christian Unity and Unity for All Humanity. Indianapolis: Disciples Council on Christian Unity, 2017. (Text also available at https:disciples.org/our-identity).
International Commission on English and the Liturgy. *Documents on the Liturgy, 1969–1979: Conciliar, Papal, and Curial Texts.* Collegeville, MN: The Liturgical Press, 1982.
Jacob, Michelle M. *Yakama Rising: Indigenous Cultural Revitalization, Activism, and Healing.* Tucson, AZ: University of Arizona Press, 2013.
Jarman, William Jackson. "A Disciples of Christ Critique: *Encounter* 24, no. 3 (Summer, 1963), 328–329.
Jones, Paul H. *Christ's Eucharistic Presence: A History of the Doctrine.* New York: Peter Lang, 1994.
Keifert, Patrick R. *Welcoming the Stranger: A Public Theology of Worship and Evangelism.* Minneapolis: Fortress Press, 1992.
Kelley, Dean M. "Is Religion a Dependent Variable?" In *Understanding Church Growth and Decline,* edited by Dean

R. Hoge and David A. Roozen. New York: Pilgrim Press, 1979.

Kinnamon, Katharine, and Iben Gjerding (eds.). *No Longer Strangers: A Resource for Women and Worship.* Geneva, Switzerland: World Council of Churches Publications, 1982.

Langer, Susanne K. *Feeling and Form: A Theory of Art Developed from Philosophy in a New Key.* New York: Charles Scribner's Sons, 1953.

_____. *Philosophical Sketches: A Study of the Human Mind in Relation to Feeling, Explored through Art, Language, and Symbol.* New York: A Mentor Book, 1964.

_____. *Philosophy in a New Key: A Study in the Symbolism of Reason, Rite and Art.* New York: A Mentor Book, 1951.

_____. (ed.) *Reflections on Art: A Source Book of Writings by Artists, Critics, and Philosophers.* New York: A Galaxy Book, 1961.

Leeuw, G. van der. *Religion in Essence and Manifestation.* New York: Harper Torchbook, 1963.

Marx, Michael (ed.). *Protestants and Catholics on the Spiritual Life.* Collegeville, MN: The Liturgical Press, 1965.

Mather, Increase. *Brief Discourse Concerning the Unlawfulness of the Common Prayer Worship.* Cambridge, UK, 1686.

McAvoy, Jane. *Table Talk: Resources for the Communion Meal.* St. Louis: Chalice Press, 1993.

McGregor, Douglas. *The Human Side of Enterprise.* New York: McGraw-Hill, 1960.

McKiernan-Allen, Linda. *We Worship in Spirit and in Truth.* St. Louis: Christian Board of Publication, 1988.

Moore, Gerard Francis. "The Eucharistic Theology of the Prayers for the Communion Service of the Lord's Supper of the Christian Church (Disciples of Christ), 1953–1987." Unpublished dissertation, The Catholic University of America, 1989.

Moore, Gerard. *The Disciples at the Lord's Table: Prayers Over Bread and Cup Across 150 Years of Christian Church (Disciples of Christ) History.* Eugene, OR: Pickwick Publications, 2015.

Morgan, Peter M. *Story Weaving: Using Stories to Transform Your Congregation.* St. Louis: Christian Board of Publication, 1986.

Morgenthaler, Sally Morgenthaler. *Worship Evangelism: Inviting*

Unbelievers into the Presence of God. Grand Rapids, MI: Zondervan Publishing, 1995.

Morrison, Charles Clayton. *The Unfinished Reformation.* New York: Harper & Brothers, 1953.

New Zealand Prayer Book, London: Collins Liturgical Publications, 1989.

Nichols, William. *Ecumenism and Catholicity.* London, UK: S.C.M. Press, 1952.

Niebuhr, H. Richard. *The Purpose of the Church and Its Ministry.* New York: Harper & Row, 1956.

Osborn, G. Edwin (ed.). *Christian Worship: A Service Book.* St. Louis: Christian Board of Publication, 1953.

Osborn, G. Edwin. "Disciples Are Learning to Worship," 9. Found in the Cole Library of the Disciples Seminary Foundation, Claremont, CA, n.d.

Osborn, Ronald E. Osborn. "Disciples and Union Among Denominations." *Shane Quarterly* 16 (1955): 108–119

_____. *In Christ's Place: Christian Ministry in Today's World.* St. Louis: Bethany Press, 1967.

_____. "Problems of Disciple Participation in the Ecumenical Movement." *Shane Quarterly* 15 (1954): 16–20.

Paul, Robert S. "British Congregational Critique." *Encounter* 24, no. 3 (Summer 1963), 318–320.

Power, David N. "The Eucharistic Prayer: Another Look." In *New Eucharistic Prayers: An Ecumenical Study of Their Development and Structure,* edited by Frank C. Senn, 239–257. Mahwah, NJ: Paulist Press, 1987.

Reumann, John. "A History of Lectionaries: From the Synagogue at Nazareth to Post Vatican II." *Interpretation* 31, no. 2 (April 1977): 131–138.

Richardson, William J. Richardson. "Toward Christian Unity." Addresses given at the Oregon Christian Missionary Convention, 1951.

Robinson, William. *Essays on Christian Unity.* London, UK: James Clarke and Co., 1922.

_____. *The Administration of the Lord's Supper.* Birmingham, UK: The Berean Press, 1947; reprinted, 1959.

_____. *What Churches of Christ Stand For.* Birmingham, UK: The Berean Press, 1946.

Rose-Heim, William B. *Baptism and Belonging: A Study Guide.* Indianapolis: Division of Homeland Ministries, Christian Church (Disciples of Christ), 1992.

Rowell, J. Cy. *Thankful Praise: A Study Guide.* St. Louis: Christian Board of Publication, 1987.

Rudolph, L. C. *Hoosier Faiths: A History of Indiana Churches and Religious Groups.* Bloomington, IN: Indiana University Press, 1995.

Schleiermacher Friedrich. *The Christian Faith,* translated by H. R. McIntosh and J. S. Stewart. Edinburgh, Scotland: T.&T. Clark, 1928.

Schmidt. Leigh Eric, *Holy Fairs: Scottish Communions and American Revivals in the Early Modern Period.* Princeton, NJ: Princeton University Press, 1989.

Schwartz, Rudolf. *The Church Incarnate: The Sacred Function of Church Architecture.* Chicago: Henry Regnery Company, 1958.

Shands, Alfred R. *The Liturgical Movement and the Local Church* (rev. ed.). New York: Morehouse-Barlow Co., 1965.

Shelton, Orman L. *The Church Functioning Effectively.* St. Louis: Christian Board of Publication, 1946.

Shepherd, Massey H. Shepherd, Jr. "An Anglican Critique." *Encounter* 24, no. 3 (Summer 1963), 323–324.

Stuart, George. "The Disciples and Evanston." *The Christian-Evangelist* 92, no. 10 (March 10, 1954): 223–224.

Stuhlman, Byron D. *Eucharistic Celebration, 1789–1979* New York: Church Hymnal Corporation, 1988.

The Problem and Method of Prayer Book Revision. Prayer Books Studies 15. New York: The Church Pension Fund, 1961.

Toler, Thomas W. *The Elder at the Lord's Table.* St. Louis: Bethany Press, 1954.

Turner, Victor. *The Forest of Symbols: Aspects of Ndembu Ritual.* Ithaca, NY: Cornell University Press, 1970; originally published, 1967.

Underhill, Evelyn. *Worship.* Eugene, OR: Wipf and Stock, 2002.

Wainwright, Geoffrey. *Doxology: The Praise of God in Worship, Doctrine, and Life.* New York: Oxford University Press, 1980.

Watkins, Keith. *A Visible Sign of God's Presence: A History of the Yakama Christian Mission.* Bethany, WV: Disciples of Christ Historical Society and Polar Star Press, 2009.

———. "An Order of Holy Communion for Use Every Sunday." *Encounter* 24, no. 3 (Summer 1963): 303–309.

———. *Celebrate with Thanksgiving: Patterns of Prayer at the Communion Table.* St. Louis: Chalice Press, 1991

———. "Disciples of Christ in Ecumenical Encounter." B.Div. thesis, Butler University, 1956.
———. Interview with Leon Riley. October 1, 2001.
———. *Liturgies in a Time When Cities Burn.* Nashville, TN: Abingdon Press, 1969.
———. "Liturgy and the Free Church," *Encounter* 23, no. 2 (Spring 1962). 193–203.
———. "Shifting Left/Shifting Right: Changing Eucharistic Practices in Churches of the Stone-Campbell Tradition." *Discipliana* 56, no. 2 (Summer 1996): 35–48.
———. (ed.). *Thankful Praise: A Resource for Christian Worship.* St. Louis: Christian Board of Publication, 1987.
———. *The American Church that Might Have Been: A History of the Consultation on Church Union.* Eugene, OR: Wipf and Stock, 2015.
———. *The Breaking of Bread: An Approach to Worship for the Christian Churches (Disciples of Christ).* St. Louis: Bethany Press, 1966.
———. *The Communion Service: A Model for the Christian Church (Disciples of Christ).* Indianapolis: Division of Homeland Ministries, Christian Church (Disciples of Christ), 1983.
———. *The Ecclesiastical Contributions of Increase Mather to Late Seventeenth and Early Eighteenth Century Puritan Thought.* Berkeley, CA: Pacific School of Religion, 1964.
———. *The Feast of Joy: The Lord's Supper in Free Churches.* St. Louis: Bethany Press, 1977.
———. *The Great Thanksgiving: The Eucharistic Norm of Christian Worship.* St. Louis: Chalice Press, 1995.
———. "The Sacramental Character of the Camp Meeting." *Discipliana* 54, no. 1 (Spring 1994): 2–19.
———. "Twenty Years with the Consultation on Church Union." *Mid-Stream* 34, no. 3 (July/October 1995): 93–103
———. "Vision-Driven Ministry: Reflections on Atlanta's Perimeter Church and Perimeter Ministries International." *Encounter* 56, no. 3 (Summer 1995): 289–309.
Watkins, Sharon. *Whole: A Call to Unity in Our Fragmented World.* St. Louis: Chalice Press, 2014.
Wedel, Theodore. "The Theology of the Liturgical Movement." In *The Liturgical Renewal of the Church*, edited by Massey H. Shepherd Jr., 3–5. New York: Oxford University Press, 1960.

Wicker, Brian. "Ritual and Culture: Some Dimensions of the Problem Today. In *The Roots of Ritual*, edited by James Shaughnessy, 13-45. Grand Rapids, MI: Eerdmans, 1973.

Wilburn, Ralph G. "A Critique of the Restoration Principle: Its Place in Contemporary Life and Thought." *Encounter* 20, no. 3 (Summer 1959): 333–361.

Williams, D. Newell. *Barton Stone: A Spiritual Biography.* St. Louis: Chalice Press, 2000.

Wilson, Josh L. Jr. (ed.). "A Recital of the Mighty Acts of God: An Order for Christian Meeting and Thanksgiving." Berkeley, CA: The Christian Churches of Northern California-Nevada, 1962.

Winter, Gibson. *The Suburban Captivity of the Churches: An Analysis of Protestant Responsibility in the Expanding Metropolis.* Garden City, NJ: Doubleday, 1961.

Wolfe, Michael C. "The Growth and Decline of the Christian Church (Disciples of Christ) in Los Angeles County: What Could Our Future Be?" Unpublished professional project, Claremont School of Theology, 1983.

Woodward, William W. *Surprising Accounts of the Revival of Religion; In the United States of America, in Different Parts of the World, and Among Differen[t] Denominations.* In American Christianity (vol. 1), edited by H. Shelton Smith, Robert T. Handy, and Lefferts A. Loetscher, 566–570. New York: Charles Scribner's Sons, 1960.

World Council of Churches. *Baptism, Eucharist, and Ministry.* Geneva, Switzerland: World Council of Churches, 1982.

Wuthnow, Robert. *The Restructuring of American Religion: Society and Faith Since World War II.* Princeton, NJ: Princeton University Press, 1988.

www.ingramcontent.com/pod-product-compliance
Lightning Source LLC
Chambersburg PA
CBHW071003160426
43193CB00012B/1898